The Man Who Became Santa Claus,

And Other Winter Tales

The Man Who Became Santa Claus,

And Other Winter Tales

By Lorraine Ahearn

Cold Type
PRESS

The Man Who Became Santa Claus, and Other Winter Tales

Copyright © 2010 by Lorraine Ahearn

Illustrations copyright © 2010 by John Hitchcock

Published by Cold Type Press
Greensboro, North Carolina

Visit our website at www.lorraineahearn.com

Printed in the United States of America

Edwards Brothers, Inc.,
Ann Arbor, Michigan

First Printing: October 2009

Edited by Mike Kernels

Book design by Elaine Shields

ISBN 978-0-692-00535-4

In memory of my father,
Guy J. Ahearn

CONTENTS

❄

PART 3 – Cold War Stories

PART 4 – Game Faces

PART 5 – The Eve of St. Agnes, the Shortest Day of the Year

PART 6 – Christmas Morning

The Cold Ink of Clarity

❄

I was born, like my father, in a cold month. This explains why my axis tilts naturally to winter, a season, as Garrison Keillor wrote, "when nature is trying to kill you."

Not that Dad didn't worship summer, bask in it, bake in it. But like a guest around a motel pool, he was just a tourist passing through. Winter was terra firma, the indelible imprint on his DNA. Gray skies, bare woods, icy streams run in our veins, a chip off some craggy, god-forsaken west Irish cliff that Dad's forebears had the good sense to forsake.

But year after year, Christmas and its requisite merriment seemed a paradox in our house. The lyrics spoke of comfort and joy, but the notes rang off-key. As a rib roast sputtered in the oven and a Nat King Cole LP caramelized on the stereo, my Italian mother painted a gilded Madonna and Child freehand on the picture window facing the street. On an end table, we kids arranged a manger with a Baby Jesus bathed in a blue light bulb's glow.

Meanwhile, my father would fall into a far-off, unreachable reverie at Christmas. The reason remained a mystery we would not unlock for many a year. Come to think of it, I never understood it until my father was gone, and as a newspaper columnist, I happened to interview his old World War II sergeant, sole living survivor from Dad's 82nd Airborne unit. Come to find out, as recounted in Part 3's "Cold War Stories," that Christmas carols, deep snow drifts and mangers held altogether different memories for those who lived through one particular Christmas night in the Ardennes Forest. Needless to say, they were not memories of comfort and joy. On the other hand, his old sergeant seemed joyful enough now to be sitting comfortably by an indoor tree, with a toy manger and ceramic animals.

In my 12 years as a metro columnist for the News & Record, and 16 before that as a reporter, the stories of how people like them not only survived these grievous hours, but became stronger and more human as a result, have been the bigger mystery. They make journalism a mission akin to (dare I say?) religion, a lens that shows the world in a new light.

The first story in this book, "Baby Jane Doe," is the first column I wrote for the newspaper in trying out for the job. Subsequently, every December from 1998 to 2008, as days grew shorter and we approached the solstice, I have borrowed a Tet tradition from my Chinese and Vietnamese friends. That is, I tried to settle all debts with my editors by way of our annual "Winter People" series, from which many of the following true stories are taken.

Still, why winter?

Nell Lewis, who was gardening columnist for the former Greensboro Daily News when I joined the paper as an obituary writer back in college, once called this season "nature's x-ray." Winter, Lewis explained, allows the gardener to see straight to the structure of things, without the leaves of spring, summer or fall obstructing the view. The same, I would argue, can be said of human adversity. When circumstances are easy, when roses bloom, birds sing and the sun shines, who knows our true essence? Yet when our backs are to the wall, we look in the mirror and behold our true selves – for better, for worse.

The people in these pages are in the winter of the year, faces etched in the cold ink of clarity. The comfort they offer is in strength. The joy, against gray skies and bare woods, derives from within.

Lorraine Ahearn
Greensboro, North Carolina

Winter, 2009

PART 1

What Child is This?

Baby Jane Doe:
"We Are Her Family"

❄

It seemed awkward and futile, but no more so than any other burial.

People stood hushed and waiting, squinting in the afternoon sun, dress shoes sinking into the wet ground. Slowly, the coffin was lowered with the utmost care and ceremony – a cushioned casket encased in a metal vault, to protect it from the elements.

Too much care, you might argue, and too late.

But this wasn't like most burials. The folding metal chairs arranged under the funeral tent for family members were empty. So was the stretch limousine riding behind the hearse carrying an unclaimed baby to a donated grave.

Following behind on the way to Maplewood Cemetery Sunday were 70 cars in a motorcade of strangers, part of a spontaneous outpouring of sympathy in the two weeks since the child's body was found in a trash bin in Greensboro.

Amid that groundswell – offers of flowers, help from every undertaker in town, even a lullaby written for "Baby Jane Doe" and performed at Sunday's funeral – some people had been wondering privately if it wasn't too much, too late.

Granted, this uneasy argument went, the baby's death

was tragic and highly symbolic. But what about all the children among us who still need help – who are neglected, abused, unloved?

Why not ask Geneva McIntyre, a detective in the Greensboro Police Youth Division? This is, after all, her case.

McIntyre was the one standing watch over the baby's casket Sunday as strangers lined up to pay their respects at Glenwood Community Center. She has worked in the youth division since 1989, and still thinks back to a sex abuse case she investigated early on – a 9-month-old baby victim. Having a pretty good idea who did it, but not enough evidence to go to court.

"You have to lay down at night," she said, "and a lot of times you will see what you've been dealing with all day."

Around the walls of the community center stood fellow detectives who volunteered to work the funeral, and in the front row sat Dr. Jan Hessling, Guilford County Medical Examiner.

Hessling, like Detective McIntyre, doesn't operate in a world of teddy bears and flowers. She is paid to cast a cold eye on death, to size up details down to the millimeter.

But after visiting the crime scene on a chilly January morning, she got a call from the driver responsible for transporting the body, asking who was going to bury the baby. Hessling decided she would have to be responsible, and bought the child a burial gown.

Thus, the baby's death linked several people whose paths crossed the day she was found.

The coroner's driver came along with a second pallbearer, the old man who discovered the baby's body while looking for aluminum cans. The neighbor who lives closest to the park where the baby was found sat on a back bleacher during the service, eyes closed, a hand to her forehead. At the cemetery, she walked away wearily as the coffin was covered with dirt.

For them, the baby's death wasn't symbolic. It was personal. And the motorcade, the flowers, the lullaby, it was all too late.

But the alternative? It might be to live in a city where an unclaimed baby's death isn't news anymore, just a back-page item to scan over and shake your head at. Tragic, a highly symbolic sign of the times, to be sure, but nothing you can't get used to.

In that sense, Sunday's service wasn't futile, if only as a reminder that there is room at the inn. It doesn't have to happen this way.

And although this must have been the hundredth funeral the Rev. Julie Peeples has presided over, and although she knew all the right things to say, when the minister reached the end of the burial, and there was nothing left to do, even she seemed lost.

"It is customary at a burial for the minister to greet the family," Peeples said, turning from the empty metal chairs and looking to the crowd that encircled the grave.

"We are her family."

— February 17, 1997

The Foundling, Eight Years Later: Whose Son Is He?

❋

The hospital won't discharge a baby without a name, they told the foster mother, and her first choice was Payne.

She liked the sound of it, but the social worker didn't. Seeing as how the newborn boy was left in a sink of an office building restroom one freezing morning, Payne had, well ... bad connotations.

So they pulled some other name out of a hat, and home Payne went to his foster family. And that was always the thing about this baby. How he clung to her right away, how his eyes followed her around the room. As if he knew he was home.

The lady who found him in the sink said the same thing. Mazelle Moore had just unlocked the Greensboro NAACP office on East Market, hadn't even put the coffee on, when she heard this infant's wail – from the doctor's office down the hall, she assumed, or the Black Child Development Institute.

But as she went to fill her coffee pot, Moore realized it was coming from the women's room – a tiny, naked boy, blue-green from the cold, left in the porcelain sink. And from the moment she flipped the light on to the time the rescue truck took him away, Moore never heard him cry again. As if he knew he'd been found.

Well, all that is almost eight years ago, and now the boy is tall. The first year or so, they do every test in the book. Negative for drug traces, negative for HIV, no lasting damage from the severe hypothermia.

They even measure his head every three months, and by the time the foster mother adopts him outright at age two, the doctors know everything about him you can know about a child. Except for who he is.

His mother has known this day was coming, when he would pose the question, but when he finally does, it catches her off guard. They're out shopping, in the middle of Kmart.

Am I adopted, Mom?

That's right, she tells him. So are two of his siblings, one half Asian and half black, another Hispanic, and the adoptive mother white. That leads him to another question.

What color am I?

A beautiful hot chocolate color, she tells him, and he's satisfied for a while. Until they're at some event celebrating "multiculturalism," and everybody's supposed to stick a pin on the map marking where their cultural roots lie. Europe, Mexico, Vietnam, Africa.

What am I? he whispers to her. And she pulls one out of a hat: You're Afghani.

Then again, who knows? He's lean and light-skinned, with silky hair and a strong, angular jaw. Bright eyes, happy, good-natured, liked by everyone. He lays his clothes out at night before school, to make sure his pants match his shirt. He sucked his thumb as a child, but has learned to tuck it under his pillow to break the habit.

Lately he's pressed for more details about his adoption. You have got the most unusual story, his mother begins. You were found in a sink...

There's little more to tell. The police kept the case open for more than a year, but the only clues were a white thermal undershirt found with the baby, and a report that somebody maybe saw a man going out the back door of the office building that morning.

Lt. T.R. Bellamy, then a youth detective, asked around at hospitals and student infirmaries, looking for women who had been noticeably pregnant but weren't anymore. Someone gave the name of a crack addict, but he found her in a hospital, with her baby. About the same time, Bellamy was assigned to investigate when a city crew found the body of a fully-developed baby flushed down the sewage system.

And as for the boy they almost named Payne? He turns 8 this February, and there will be three women who remember his birthday. The lady who found him, the mother who gave him a home, and the woman who knows how his story began, but missed out on all the rest.

— December 24, 2000

What Child Stirs Under the Stairs?

❄

The baby was found wrapped in a bed sheet with cartoon figures from the kids' movie "Anastasia."

You know, the one about the Russian child princess who escapes a firing squad, but as a result grows up an obscure pauper with no claim to her royal identity.

Anyway, make what you will of the child's bed sheet, Greensboro police Detective Ruth Woodard was saying the other day. Maybe that solitary shred of a clue means whoever had the baby and left her under the apartment stairwell already had children and didn't want this one.

Or maybe it means someone had been getting ready for this baby all along, but had a change of heart at the last minute and decided the baby would be better off with strangers.

And so she was.

At 5:45 a.m. on Nov. 12, a tenant leaving for work opened the door of her apartment at Hunter's Glen on McKnight Mill Road and heard something stirring on the concrete stoop under the stairwell. It was a girl, a few hours old, the umbilical cord still attached, feeling the cold but very much alive.

And that's as much as we know about her. By the time the sun came up at the working-class apartment building a block from the Sands Motel along U.S. 29 North, TV crews were already milling around, pointing cameras at the now-empty stairwell and talking about "Baby Jane Doe."

But that was never her name, and she was long gone by that time. She was whisked off to the Intensive Care Unit at Women's Hospital, where warm lights slowly brought her temperature to normal and soft-voiced nurses hovered over her a little more than the other babies.

The nurses nicknamed her "Caroline" – she was found in the part of town close to Carolina Circle – and she had a serene disposition but a healthy set of lungs.

What else do we need to know about "Caroline?" She was 6 pounds 13 ounces – a full-term baby, the doctors said. She appears to be light-complected African-American, the police said, but that didn't narrow it down much, either: Her mother could be black, white or Hispanic.

Which is about as cold as a cold case gets. And the peculiar part is, unless someone comes forward with information, Caroline's secret is safe now – swaddled in the seamless garment of confidentiality rules.

Ask what sort of foster family she's with, and that's part of the "child protective services record." Ask about the location, and that's getting "case specific" – a taboo spelled out in a battery of state and federal chapters and verses.

"It's just so thoroughly frustrating," observes Ruth Woodard, the detective on the case. "It's not like I can broadcast her picture and ask the public, 'Does this baby favor someone you know who was recently pregnant?' "

In the same breath, Woodard's not complaining. She worked another abandoned newborn case two winters back, and you probably read all about it.

There was, in contrast, so much to tell about that

"Baby Jane Doe" – she was left in a Dumpster one cold morning, and I don't need to ask the Department of Social Services where she is today. She's over in Maplewood Cemetery with not one headstone, but two – one from a community she never got to see, another from a grandmother she never got to know.

Caroline, on the other hand, could be anybody's baby. That's how her story ends – for us, at least. A reverse Anastasia.

Except for some footsteps in the night that somebody did or didn't hear, except for a thin little bedsheet that did little to protect her from the cold, there's not much to connect her back to her first squalid hours in the world. There's no story she'll look up on microfilm at the library 20 years from now and say for certain, "That was me."

It's a stone cold whodunit. And one look in the eyes of a youth detective like Woodard, and you get the feeling there are worse things in life, things you don't even want to read about.

"I don't know what kind of chance this infant would have had with parents who would leave it under a stairwell," she says. "I'd rather have a live baby and no suspect than a dead baby and an in-custody suspect."

Maybe the case that so far didn't get solved makes more sense than the one that did.

"The child must have a purpose for it to have gone through that kind of trauma and survived," Woodard tells me. "I don't know to be ungrateful for little things."

– December 19, 1999

Living In the Lost and Found

✳

It will be 15 years this January since Abigail vanished, and they fanned out to search the woods behind the house, frantic, sleepless, wrung raw by the time a tracker traced her last footprints to the murky waters of Buffalo Creek.

She'd been missing six days, each headline plodding toward a grim conclusion. *Girl, 6, is missing.* Then, *Discouraging search for girl continues.* A glimmer of a lead: *Girl's hat found on other side of stream.* And then finally, *Deceptive bridge of trash let child slip, drown, tracker says.*

After which comes a drive to clean up the polluted, garbage-choked creek. Too late for Abigail, so these stories seem to trail off, empty-handed, futile, no matter what we say at the time to make it otherwise.

How does it happen, then, that on a sunny Friday morning nearly 15 years later, Ralph Blythe finds himself walking down the same hall of the same school where his daughter Abigail had been a first-grader when she died in 1989?

The answer is simple – to that question, anyway. It seems that Mattie, 6, adopted as a baby foundling from China, forgot her lunch when she left the house today.

So before he goes to work, Ralph retraces Mattie's steps, a 52-year-old man trying to think like a 6-year-old, and finds the lunch she dropped in the closet when she put on her coat.

Lunch in hand, he walks past rows of kindergarten artwork, bold, clumsy attempts to paint "Starry Night." He thinks about the impish, black-haired girl, a girl he calls "a caution," who will greet him at the end of the hall in Mrs. Smith's class.

He thinks about the day ahead, most of the time.

❋ ❋ ❋

Never make a major decision after something as traumatic as the death of a child. Everybody says that – the counselors, the self-help books.

But the fact is, they have to move out of this house. Morning and night, Ralph knows it's killing his wife, Vickie. There's a heaviness she can't escape, even by going outside. Especially by going outside, where the creek flows between their yard and the landfill near Carolina Circle Mall.

To think she and Ralph moved here with their two girls because it seemed safe – the end of a long dirt road, no neighbors, just woods around them.

❋ ❋ ❋

The day that it happens, younger sister Hannah, barely 2 at the time, has been up half the night before with an earache. So by the time Vickie gets home from work that afternoon, the mother needs to lay down and rest for a few minutes while Abigail, as usual, goes out to play with her Labrador puppy, Daisy.

The mother, finding the child has left her coat behind on the January day, within minutes begins looking for her. Before dusk, volunteers are combing the woods for a blond girl in a gray-blue dress, pink leg warmers, black high-top Reeboks and the blue beret she always wore, a fan of Cagney on "Cagney and Lacey."

By nightfall, a bloodhound has tracked Abigail's scent to the creek, and by 8 p.m., Daisy, the Lab puppy, comes home dripping wet, alone.

On the fifth day, Apache-trained tracker Tom Brown Jr. arrives, and by the next afternoon he leads them to the spot on the other side of the creek where the lost, panicked child tried to cross back over. The tracker points the divers to a logjam of garbage that would have looked like a bridge in the moonlight, but he leaves before they pull her out.

The child's father – haggard, anguished, drops to his knees that Sunday afternoon, right there in the woods, going not one step closer.

And that's where life stops for Ralph and Vickie. Time might flow around them, over and under them, but they're stuck in place, like a rock in a stream.

They don't talk about Abigail. Not about the day Vickie lay out there with her in the yard, looking at a perfect blue sky. Not about the night Ralph read to Abigail at bedtime and said he didn't know what he'd do if anything ever happened to her. Had he said it out loud or just thought it?

Friends bow out of the picture, not wanting to be reminded, and life becomes a numb routine. After a few weeks off, Vickie trudges back to her job as a teacher's aide, agonizing every time she has to leave her baby daughter, Hannah, at day care. Ralph, meanwhile, can't even bear the sight of an EMS truck. He throws himself into his job as a quality inspector, grateful for it.

Hannah, now an only child, looks from one parent's face to the other.

All the statistics would indicate that this is the end – the divorce rate, depression, you name it. Still, Vickie has been down this path before. As a girl, she watched her own mother withdraw, shrouded in grief, losing a husband in a car wreck and a son to a brain tumor all in one year.

Now, she's walking in her mother's shoes, and doesn't judge anymore. But she has walked in Hannah's shoes as well. There has to be another way out.

They try to have another baby, in time. Then they hear of an adoption meeting. Let's just go see, they say.

❄ ❄ ❄

In Maoming, at the southern tip of China, as in every other city in China, it's against the law for families to have more than one child.

So it happens a lot – delivery nurses in maternity wards will be cleaning up a newborn girl – typically a girl – and turn to find the mother gone, having slipped out a window or a back exit. Or babies are just left somewhere, and hopefully someone finds them.

Which is how life begins for Mao Xiao Mei, according to the adoption papers: She's left in a basket on the steps of a middle school in Maoming, only two weeks old.

By the time Ralph gets a call from the adoption agency, telling him to pick up the baby's picture, he and Vickie have been on the waiting list for two years. He rushes over to Hannah's school, where Vickie is working, and shows them the picture.

The next thing they know, the parents are half a world away, sitting in a Maoming restaurant, the waitresses too wrapped up in a TV soap opera to pay this nervous-looking American couple any attention.

Up pulls a van, a sliding door opens, and an elderly Chinese woman holds an infant on each knee.

"That one's mine," Vickie says, and just like that, she's holding the chubby baby from the photo.

Ralph is supposed to be videotaping all this, but it happens too fast.

They've got the tree up, a live tree, a little early this year. Mattie – short for Madeline – has a hint of the flu, so Vickie keeps her home Thursday. They probably worry too much.

On the other hand, Hannah has her own car – 16, pretty, smart, a great kid, but a little serious. They worry about that, too.

But nothing can be undone, no one can be replaced. The most they can do is try to fill in the empty places.

And so it was that Mattie slept in Abigail's old crib as a baby, as Hannah had before her, and wore Abigail's clothes, each size up until age 6, anyway.

It made it seem like a natural progression, the way it would have been if she hadn't died. But you know, these things only last so long – the home videos Vickie still can't watch, the little laminated evergreen ornament, with a scribble of crayon and, in some preschool teacher's pencil, "Love, Abigail."

Even Daisy, the puppy, is gone – she lived on another 10 years after the night she came home without Abigail, but finally had to be put down with a hip problem. After they all pestered Ralph, he finally went down to the pound and brought home a new puppy, a black and white Lab.

And this is how a surprising child, surviving odds of her own, helps them stay alive. She forgets her lunch. At a Skateland party, she waves, giggling, unsteady on her skates, as Vickie watches on the sidelines, wincing at the techno-pop beat.

A day earlier, Mattie has been home sick in her pajamas, plugging in the Christmas lights, fiddling with a tin foil star that's already coming apart.

She parks a favorite toy in Vickie's lap, a purple unicorn that talks when Vickie squeezes the paw.

You're braver than you think, says the voice, which makes Mattie laugh.

And no, it's not the same without Abigail. It never will be, no matter how much time smooths it over, like water over a stone.

Still, something refused to die that night on Buffalo Creek. Something good.

– December 14, 2003

Her 44-Year Secret:
The Blue Package Arrived Safely

❄

S ome other time, some other place, they might have rejoiced at the news and tied a blue ribbon to the mailbox or a balloon proclaiming, "It's a boy!"

But the only announcement of this birth would be an anonymous, long-distance phone call and the cryptic voice of a stranger talking in code to Nancy McFall's parents.

"The blue package," the voice said, "arrived safely."

It was 1959, and out-of-wedlock births were shrouded in as much secrecy as Cold War espionage. Pregnant at 16, McFall had been whisked off to a home for unwed mothers, across the state line, away from prying neighbors and relatives in the small town of South Hill, Va.

Other than her parents, she hadn't breathed a word to anyone – not her best friend, not even the father of the baby, her fiancé at the time.

Living at a Salvation Army home near Duke, she would exchange letters with her mother, but always through an address in Atlanta. There, someone would put the letter in another envelope and forward it on, lest anyone back in South Hill find out.

"It was a small town, and it thrived on gossip. That's an ugly thing to say, but it's true. There were no secrets," McFall said the other day.

"This was a sin. The worst possible sin. I would have been a bad girl, a slut. My parents said if anyone found out, my life would be ruined."

So after giving birth at Duke and getting three days to spend with her baby, McFall signed "relinquishment" papers for the child to be adopted through the Children's Home Society in Greensboro.

And then she put it behind her, supposedly. She broke things off with her fiancé, and her mother had her burn any pictures or letters the couple had shared. For years, she never attended high school reunions, for fear that someone would ask about why she left town.

She married, moved with her husband's Army career, became a nurse, had two daughters, went on with her life. But instead of the secret becoming a lighter burden, it grew heavier.

For instance, there was each Sept. 14, her son's birthday. And each time she saw a boy his age, older by the year. And the day she accompanied a married friend who was adopting a child – a boy, as fate would have it – McFall wore a frozen smile.

Finally, in the still of one evening in early 2004 at her home in Danville, Va., well after McFall's parents had taken her secret to their graves, the phone rang.

At first, she thought it was a telemarketer seeking donations. Then the name registered, crashing in on her – the Children's Home Society. The son she gave birth to 44 years ago had won a court order for the agency to call McFall. He wanted to meet his birth mother.

"To say I went all to pieces would be putting it mildly," McFall said. "I said, 'My husband, nobody in the world knows about this.' "

On the other end of the line, the voice of veteran social worker Edith Votta was calm. There was a reason McFall's son had been granted an exception to North Carolina's closed adoption law, the nation's strictest.

"He has health issues."

❄ ❄ ❄

Who knows how long he sat there staring at her picture in the yearbook – Parkview High School, Class of 1958?

Two years and $10,000 spent searching, paying private detectives, fantasizing about how this story would end, had all led Earl Moore to the public library in South Hill.

From a shelf of forgotten high school annuals people had donated, he guessed at the year, and sure enough, there was the name, below the most familiar looking stranger he had ever seen. He enlarged the picture on the library photocopier before he left.

Then he changed his mind.

"I'd like to make a donation to the library. Here's fifty bucks," he told the librarian, then tucked the yearbook under his arm and walked out, headed next to the county courthouse.

Finding the marriage license, her address, the names of her other children – all that turned out to be the easy part. The fact was, she didn't want to meet him. She had answered the health questions about their shared history of hypertension. But as for that wall erected back in 1959 when the case was sealed, McFall had no wish to remove it.

"For our health," she wrote in response to a letter Moore sent her – once again, through an intermediary –

"it would be better if we didn't communicate any further."

So this would have to do. A yearbook picture, a look at her handwriting on the marriage license, a drive by her house in Danville, just for curiosity.

What did he want from her, after all? It wasn't money. He'd been successful down in Georgia, owned a couple of Best Westerns and some Zaxby's restaurants in Asheville.

Nor did he want to shame her for giving him away. He was a big boy now. And looking back on it, the teenage girl in the yearbook photo had done the right thing. The Children's Home Society had placed him with good parents. He had a great childhood, always felt wanted.

Still, even before they told him at age 12 that he was adopted, he'd always harbored questions. He had red hair and freckles, but his mother had olive skin. His adoptive parents, long dead now, had been old enough to be his grandparents. And he never clicked with his father. They were wired differently, like an Apple and an IBM.

For adopted children such as Moore – one of an estimated 6 million in the secretive years between 1939 and 1972 – the story of the stork delivering babies isn't all that far-fetched.

"I remember being in big crowds and thinking, 'What would she look like?' It was always the great unknown. And the not knowing angered me and frustrated me."

But that was that, he figured. After he got McFall's final letter of rejection, he took the yearbook photo to a restoration artist, who made an oil painting out of it using the "unidentifying information" the adoption papers gave about his mother – her auburn hair, her hazel eyes.

Then one day, browsing on the Internet, he read an article about new research being done on the genetic bond between mothers and babies. Blood work had revealed a fact researchers at first thought couldn't be possible: For many decades after giving birth, a woman carries in her bloodstream immature white cells of her baby.

There it was – a two-way bond, the blood flowing both ways. She wasn't just a fantasy in an oil painting.

Maybe she had the same instinctive longings, the unfulfilled connection that left such a void in his life.

He mailed her one more letter, his last shot. First, he had friends critique it, and he even brought it to a psychologist to read. It was only one page, but according to the log in his computer, it took him 912 minutes and 12 revisions to write.

It was his masterpiece.

❄ ❄ ❄

She's 64 now. She nursed her father and her mother before they died. She goes to church and to the beauty parlor, keeps a tidy house, looks after her grandson in the mornings. Hers is a quiet, respectable life.

But something was never quite right, and her daughters sensed it. It was sadness, something guarded and off-limits. She started seeing a therapist in the next town over. Her parents' lingering deaths just a year apart had taken a toll, the family assumed.

The truth? The therapist's office was where Earl's letters from Georgia went. When McFall read the last one, the one he spent 912 minutes writing, she had no choice. She called. They talked for two hours. She had to see him, even knowing her family would disown her.

Then again, there's what you know and what you fear. She tried to break it gently to her husband, Mac, then just blurted it out, 44 years of anguish spilling out at once.

Compose yourself, he told her.

"I am not going to 'compose' myself. I have been composed for 44 years," she answered. "I'm through with the lies and the secrets."

Between sobs, she heard something.

"Nancy," her husband said. "Nothing has changed."

He even goes with her to the meetings at the Children's Home Society in Greensboro, like the one last week where they screened "Loggerheads," the new movie set in North Carolina, about a biological mother struggling against the arcane, vault-tight state laws to locate her birth son.

And for once, the real-life story turns out better than the movie. They take vacations together, talk on the phone every day, though at first, Earl didn't know what to call Nancy McFall. "I don't care what you call me," she said, "so long as you call."

Two weeks ago, Earl Moore had a heart attack – a mild one, with a good prognosis. His wife happened to be out of town. Scared, he dialed the number in Danville.

"I just wanted to talk to my mama," he said.

She and Mac were getting in the car. He shouldn't worry. They would be right down.

– October 16, 2005

PART 2

Better than to Receive

The Man
Who Became Santa Claus

❄

For the first time in 15 Decembers, he walked into
Four Seasons Town Centre incognito last Saturday
night – no Santa Claus suit and cap, no red velvet
sack slung over his back.

With somebody else sitting in his old seat, now that
the mall has changed hands, he walked all three levels
in anonymity, taking in the crowds, the gleaming window displays, the buzz of anticipation in the place.

But then it happened, as he stood waiting for an ele-
vator, peering down from the top level at a school group
performing. Somebody looked up, another person point-
ed, and the word spread.

It's him! He's here!

And quick as a jack rabbit, the 70ish man with the
flowing white beard and round spectacles was out the
nearest exit and into the night.

His favorite table at CiCi's Pizza is smack under the
big TV. It's the quietest, least conspicuous spot in the
restaurant – everyone else sits a few tables back so they
can look up at the screen.

But it happens anyway, before he can eat his first
slice. A little girl, 7 years old, sits staring at him from
across the crowded restaurant, as if they're the only two
people in the place – her and this old man in a red shirt,

with a bald head and a crown of white hair to match his beard.

Finally, she comes over.

"Are you Santa Claus ?" she says. "I told my mama you're Santa, but she doesn't believe me."

"Well," he confides, as if she's the only one in on the secret, "I'm not wearing my uniform right now ..."

He's got a reddish complexion and wears the impish, expectant look of a man who has just told a joke and is waiting for the listener to get it.

He sounds like the actor Wilford Brimley. His accent is somewhere south of Chicago, where he was born during the Depression, and somewhere north of the Everglades, where his father moved them in 1948, in time for a hurricane to flood their house, which sat between a snake farm and an abandoned orange grove.

His hands are hard and calloused from a life of labor – fixing cars, painting, doing carpentry, working as a foreman at a nuclear power plant. How he came to let his hair and beard grow out is a long story, but the way it ends is that one day he spotted a classified ad: "Santa Wanted."

He went down to Four Seasons, and after watching one skinny applicant after another audition in front of a photographer, he went up to the table.

"I've been waiting for you," the photographer said.

❄ ❄ ❄

Somebody at the TV station must have thought it was a good idea. Get the Santa from Four Seasons and put him on the air for 48 minutes, taking calls from local children. It'll be cute. Won't it?

Well, it doesn't take 48 minutes for the switchboard

to light up, and not from children calling. Santa is not only politically incorrect – he's dangerous. The adults are furious. The TV brass is furious. Whose hare-brained idea was this, anyway?

His first mistake is to tell the truth. There are lots of Santas, he tells a child caller. Sure. The world's too big for one Santa to deliver all those toys.

His second mistake is that he won't lie. No, Rudolph does not have a red nose that glows. He's a wild animal.

But really, anyone who had visited Santa at Four Seasons – and that included some-thing like 12,000 children every year – shouldn't have been surprised at the 1998 call-in show. He had been doing the unthink-able for some time – that is, talking about what hap-pened on the first Christmas and ask-ing children to sing "Happy Birthday" before opening their presents.

"You're playing with fire," a marketing director once warned him, "and you're going to get burned."

But a funny thing happened. Attendance went up at Santa's Village. It seemed the word had gotten to the churches. A mall Santa was talking about Christmas, of all things.

And the strange alchemy that occurred every time he put on the red coat didn't stop there. People started giving him things, and whether because he was a pack rat, a fix-it man or a child of the Depression, he never turned anything down.

And so it was that one year when a child asked only for a tool box for storing his bicycle tools, Santa produced one. Another boy told him that he wanted a trick bike – a very expensive bike – and Santa took the boy's father aside. If the man came back the next day, he told the father, there would be a trick bike waiting – all it needed was a new chain.

"Cool," the father said.

One Christmas, Santa found himself in possession of a piano and delivered it to a girl with spina bifida who wanted to learn to play. To this day, he can picture how her parents' faces looked when he backed the truck into their driveway.

Still, the day he remembers best was visiting an elementary school in High Point and handing out coloring books. One child handed hers back: "I don't have any crayons."

Santa questioned the girl's teacher, who said that was possible – the girl didn't seem to have anything. Later, he came back to the school and asked the teacher to bring the girl to the door of the classroom.

She looked frightened – "beaten-down," in his words – as if afraid she had done something wrong. She took the gift from him and had to be told to tear it open.

"We're not going to save the paper," he told her.

Inside was one of those Crayola anniversary sets, still in the shrink-wrap, with the gold crayon, the silver one, the works. The girl's jaw dropped. Her classmates said, "Ooooh." Santa blew a kiss and left.

❄ ❄ ❄

They didn't know his name or how to find him, and he only knew them as "the Lister Brothers." Which wasn't their real name, just what the elves at Four Seasons called them because they always brought a list.

"Oh, my God, the Lister Brothers are here again," the staff would say as the pair of tow-headed boys waited their turn in line.

This year the family came back to Four Seasons to bring Santa a letter, but he was gone. So they left the envelope at the photographer's counter, and he picked it up last Saturday night. Inside was a card with a half-dozen pictures of the boys with Santa – from pre-school to adolescence. "Thank you," the card said, "for making all our childhood Christmases magical."

True, someone else might be wearing the red suit and sitting in the chair, but there was only one Santa.

Even when he's incognito, children pick him out of a crowd, by some unseen Santa radar. Rather than breaking the spell, sighting him in civilian clothes makes them believe that much harder. Santa's not just a store employee who goes off duty at 9 p.m. He's a real guy.

And the thing about magic is that it makes anything possible. Which is how a man who answered an ad for a mall Santa turned into the real guy. With or without the red suit.

– December 12, 2004

A Beanstalk Grows in Greensboro

❄

Seeing isn't believing.

No, seeing is reserved for opening night, for curtain calls and roses, and the chance to say, "I told you so."

Believing, on the other hand, comes before all that. For instance, a dry run on a waning Tuesday afternoon, when it's raining cats and dogs outside Murphey Traditional Academy near Four Seasons, where the K-5 students are rehearsing a musical of Jack and the Beanstalk called "Fee, Fi, Fo, Fum," the school's first play in many a year.

It's a surprising departure from the flavorless gruel of yearly progress reports and end-of-grade tests. And backstage, at the moment, it's also a mob scene. Director Debbie Hunter, the fourth-grade language arts teacher who pitched this idea back in the salad days of summer vacation, now faces a grim reality.

The show is four nights away. Some students don't know their lines. A few lead actors didn't show up for rehearsal. The roof over the stage is about to spring a leak. A file cabinet that won't be moved from the wings sticks out like a sore thumb. There are more than enough cast members – 40 or 50 – to stage an uprising.

Hunter, wearing a thin smile, peeks through the curtain and spies a welcome sight. Natalie Marcle, third-grade language arts, former Teacher of the Year, a formidable presence, has entered the cafeteria.

"Marcle, are you staying?" Hunter asks, and her co-worker nods. "Thank the Lord. You got your whistle?"

Marcle blows her whistle. The stage falls silent. The show will go on.

And this is where imagination has gotten us.
Empty stomachs and no place to call home.
- Jack Spriggins' mother,
from "Fee, Fi, Fo, Fum"

The question they were all asked at Salem College was, "Can any child learn?" It was a trick question. The grad students in education, Debbie Hunter among them, were supposed to answer, no, some children simply cannot learn.

Once the grad students fell for the trap, it would snap shut. Of course every child can learn, was the correct answer. A teacher's job is to find the means.

At Murphey, Hunter's first and only full-time classroom assignment, every smug, middle-class label she had heard applied on "Title I schools," "underachieving schools" was torn away.

Yes, Murphey's students come from disadvantaged backgrounds, two-thirds qualifying for free and reduced-priced lunches, and the school has a fair-sized "S.K.I.P." program. That stands for "Save Kids of Incarcerated Parents."

But month after month, the school ranks number one or two in attendance for county elementary schools. This past week, the Salvation Army food drive would see the cafeteria lined with boxes of donated food – students bringing an average of five cans each, principal Rich

Thomae observes.

And night after night, as the stop-and-start rehearsals run longer, way longer than scheduled, parents and grandparents wait patiently in the Murphey cafeteria at the end of their workday.

"This is the first time they've ever done something like this," Bridget Beidari, whose fifth-grade daughter Bria plays Jack's mother, is saying, as she waits to coach her daughter on delivering her lines.

Around Thanksgiving of Hunter's first year of teaching, she began to notice the effect of reader's theater in the classroom. Using bits of paper, she had the students act out parts of a feast – a potato, a piece of pie, a pumpkin, and watched the words come alive off the page.

Art teacher Naomi Keltz-Jones, who helped students create sets for "Murpheytown" and a giant's castle from corrugated cardboard, agrees:

"It's sneaky. They're acting, they're painting, they're learning movement and speech. And," she jokes, "we yell at them a lot. That way they know they're learning."

Gradually, as Friday night's performance draws closer, fellow teachers begin to see it. The Latin teacher is in charge of the lights and stage-manages the cow. The speech teacher pinch-hits for missing actors. The main office registrar steps in as enforcer.

And when the first-grader "magic beans" cannot calm themselves after a madcap Tom and Jerry-style interlude, it's up to Marcle, Teacher of the Year and drill sergeant, to restore order.

"First GRADE! On the STAGE! What were you DOING?"

"RUNNING!"

"What were you told not to DO?"

"RUN!"

"Back up the STEPS. To do WHAT?"

"WALK!"

"Ms. Marcle," Hunter says, "You and I are going to get a steak when this is all through."

"I'm going to need something stronger than that," Marcle quips, then remembers the students within earshot. "Grilled onions, maybe."

"Think of the possibilities. Anyone can have money.
But magic beans are something special."
                                        - Jack Spriggins,
                                          from "Fee, Fi, Fo, Fum"

There are students that a real teacher walks through fire for, but they're not the "A" students. At least, they might not start out that way. Where's the challenge in that?

Forget about the money teachers spend out of pocket to put on a show like "Fee, Fi, Fo, Fum." Forget, even, about the evenings and the Saturdays, the e-mails, phone calls, reminders sent home, Xerox copies, permission forms.

This is a matter of faith. Not the Jesus kind. Faith in the students at Murphey. Then again, one conversation with school president Dominique Barringer, 11, and it becomes clear this is not blind faith.

Barringer, a fifth-grader, plays the sheriff. Confident, self-possessed, he could really be sheriff, if he were taller. Better yet, attorney general.

"I'm kind of nervous onstage, but I try not to look nervous. It helps to know my lines," Barringer says. "I've liked all the compliments, and enjoyed the chance to be an actor."

There is camaraderie among the cast – they give each other a silent thumbs up in the halls. As they get down to the dress rehearsal, the production numbers go smoothly at last – the show-stopping "Wiggle-Waggle," the extravagant "Market Day," and the calypso strains of "Magic Beans," when the cryptic character of the Bean Seller appears.

She is played by Ke'Avia Artis, who understands the character completely, practicing in front of the mirror at night. With Jack's family facing eviction, the Bean Seller persuades Jack to barter the family milk cow for five beans – magic beans that, sure enough, grow into giant beanstalks allowing Jack to slay the giant and save the day.

"I feel like the Bean Seller is really magical because I made the beans," says Artis, a third-grader who wants to be an actress or a singer.

"I used to believe in fairy tales. Now, I feel like I get a second chance to be what I dream."

Her favorite line comes after Jack's mother, disgusted at his barter, throws the beans in the dirt, and suddenly a great rumbling occurs and green stepladders turn into giant bean stalks, reaching through corrugated cardboard clouds.

"What did I tell you? Magic Beans?"

Sure enough, just as the Bean Seller foretold, Friday's performance would be a smash hit, standing room only. The punch lines from Erica Smalley's troll would pop like fireworks. The giant's outlandish kitchen boys would sail over the top. Missy Nicholson, the music teacher, would conjure pure sorcery from the chorus, each musical number barreling through like a runaway train. And Jack would remember his lines. They would see.

Ah, but all of this was to unfold 24 hours later. For the moment, all we have is Debbie Hunter's word for it, and she has done all she can do to make us believe. So as the last first-grader is picked up from the cafeteria by the last mother running late, Hunter and the art teacher pack up their scripts, their tote bags and tomorrow's lesson plans. They head for their cars, into the foggy night to order up a couple of steaks.

With grilled onions, no doubt.

— December 14, 2008

Goodbye, Miss O:
A Teacher Gets Called Up

❄

S he left for active duty in the Coast Guard last week, and in the grand scheme of things, I suppose, that was no news bulletin. It wasn't even one of those tearful shipside send-offs, where a spouse holding a child waves goodbye to the departing sailor.

After all, Chris Ostrom is single and has no children. All she had to do was find someone to take care of her cat, feed her fish, water her plants and make sure the rent gets paid on her empty Greensboro apartment.

And she's only going as far as Wilmington, with the job of processing in fellow reservists under the Homeland Security provisions.

"A paper-pusher," is how Ostrom, 37, describes the job that's called her back to the Coast Guard. After two years active duty at sea, and 15 in the reserve, she expected to have been activated all along since Sept. 11.

So you might say there's nothing earth-shattering in her being called up, nothing larger than life. No, it's only the ordinariness of life itself that's about to change for Chris Ostrom, and thousands like her, and anyone they might touch in the course of an ordinary day.

And when you're a seventh-grade teacher, as Ostrom is at Our Lady of Grace Catholic School, that winds up being a lot of people. The girl in her homeroom class who asked Ostrom to sponsor her confirmation. The student who brought her yet another plate of cookies on Ostrom's last day – but isn't even in her class. The teacher coming out of retirement to fill in for Ostrom. And the boy who wanted to know: How many points shy was he from a B?

"It was that last test that did you in," Ostrom was saying as school let out a week ago Friday, when she had come back to say goodbye. "Keep it up. You'll get there."

The thing about "Miss O," as they call her, is that she's not only their teacher. She's their favorite teacher.

She goes to every basketball game, and not just home games. When they do a chapter on ancient Egypt, she has them build a mummy. And when it's time for student appreciation day, as it was a week ago, she's the one who gathers snapshots of every student, teacher and parent – Halloween parties and Christmas pageants, soccer matches, First Holy Communions – and puts on a slide show, with music, for the whole school.

"I'm glad that's over," she said, grinning, as the gym emptied out and she packed her laptop and projector screen. "But what do I do next to keep me attached to this school?"

It's only her second year at the school, and in a sense, Ostrom grew up with two-year hitches. Her father was a Coast Guard commander, and was reassigned every other year – Bangkok, Washington, D.C., and a lot of points in between.

The difference was, he took his family along. In contrast, his daughter will leave behind her life – and more commitments than meet the eye.

"It leaves a tremendous hole," said Gerri Minton, whose daughter Margaret is in Ostrom's homeroom class. "She's not unattached at all. For her to leave is very difficult, when you come down to it."

Youthful and athletic, Ostrom wore her game face when she left. She told the students that if they thought they had a lot of homework, they ought to see the assignments a yeoman first class takes home. She asked them to keep the cookies and e-mail coming, and promised to be at their last home game, against rival Pius.

 Which she was – sitting in the bleachers that Saturday morning, a day before reporting for duty. The gym was stuffy and crowded as the junior varsity boys huffed up and down the court, whistles blowing, buzzers sounding, visitors cheering as OLG missed the free throw.

Chris Ostrom hunched forward, rooting for them, keeping her mind on the game. But the truth was, her footlocker was packed and another teacher had already moved into her desk. And like a stream flowing over a rock, ordinary life had opened around her, closed again and kept rushing by.

– February 9, 2003

Small Change, and All the Pancakes You Can Eat

❄

"You get all kinds of little rewards," his boss at the pancake house tells me. "Jon, in a way, is one of them."

We're sitting here talking about the restaurant business, in the middle of the lunch rush at Tex & Shirley's. The smell of bacon, coffee and maple syrup is in the air. Plates clatter on the galley. A line of customers, most of them regulars, backs up toward the door. Next to the hostess stand, a veteran waitress watches a diner count out small change for her tip.

And a busboy named Jon Reiser takes all this in, as he does Monday through Friday, reliable as the big clock on the dining room wall.

The bus drops him off in the morning out front – a big, loping 17-year-old – almost 6 feet tall, sandy blond hair, blue eyes. He ties on a clean white apron, greets each co-worker by name, and starts busing tables, like his two older brothers before him.

Unlike his brothers, however, he has no plans for college. Jon is autistic, and this is his first job.

It's been more than a year since he took his first paycheck to the bank and made out a deposit. Sometimes customers who aren't regulars complain that he stares or talks to himself, but his co-workers just shrug. He does fine.

"I see him improve a little every day. Sometimes he moves faster than I do," says Allyson Hooker, a hostess who also buses, as Jon wipes the table in a booth. "He learned all that by watching me. It makes me feel good."

Jon is a junior at Grimsley High School, in a class of students who work part-time jobs at businesses around the city, from Libby Hill to Moses Cone Extended Care. His mother took the idea to Tex & Shirley's, telling manager Gilbert Jones that Jon would need a "job coach."

"Gilbert said, 'What the heck is a job coach?' " mother Sandy Reiser recalls. "It's somebody to teach him and make sure his job gets done. So he said, 'Sure.' "

Nothing new to Gilbert, a balding, 44-year-old manager who has been in the business 30 years. Everybody's got their flaws, Gilbert can assure you.

Take, for example, a dishwasher he trained. Close the door and push the button. Sometimes the man closed the door and didn't push the button, or pushed the button and didn't close the door, leaving Gilbert soaking wet. Then he learned.

For Jon, who is training at a data entry job at UNCG, and a job filling telephone orders at a family-owned grocery, this won't be the only chance in the working world. The thing is, it was his first chance.

That was the day his mother had to step back. Like when you finally take the training wheels off the bike, or let go of the wriggling body when you're standing in the deep water. Step back, hold your breath, and watch him go in whatever direction he'll be going a long time after you're gone.

It's already happening, she thinks, in a circle now reaching beyond the security of his school or his backyard gate. The circle changes Jon a little, but listen hard behind the clatter of the Friday lunch rush, and you hear Jon change the circle, too.

Not that the tips are getting any bigger for waitress Linda Marshall, who's waited tables here for 17 years. Not that Gilbert Jones' knees probably hurt any less after a 12-hour day.

But behind the monotonous hum of the dining room, Jon makes things less routine. When co-worker Allyson turned 30, he made her a birthday card on his computer, one card she'll keep. For a homework assignment on Thanksgiving, listing what he's thankful for, Jon put down his job at Tex & Shirley's. Gilbert felt like posting that one over the time clock.

Every morning Jon greets each co-worker one by one, and one by one says goodbye every afternoon. Often he'll tell a female customer, "You look pretty" – words a lot of these customers haven't heard from a 17-year-old boy since they were 17 themselves.

And he checks his watch every couple of minutes, never mind the big clock on the wall, to see if it's time. At 1 p.m. every day – no earlier, no later – Allyson will bring him a tall iced tea and a hot, heaping plate of pancakes. He doesn't even have to order – why would he order anything else?

He sits at a table in the back dining room and carefully adds syrup – never butter – and intently cuts the pancake stacks into triangular sections that soak up the syrup.

You get all kinds of little rewards, Jon's boss was telling me. And Jon, in a way, is one of them.

– January 11, 1998

Extended Life of a Salesman

❄

As far as anybody knows, he's the last door-to-door salesman in Greensboro, other than those men on bicycles peddling salvation.

But all Luther Clegg promises is satisfaction or your money back. Climbing a customer's front steps, he carries samples – Never Dull metal cleaner and Guaranteed brand extended-life light bulbs, all packed in a leather suitcase with a broken buckle and duct tape around the corners.

"My old one was a lot worse," says Clegg, 85, a Greensboro native who went to work as a Fuller Brush salesman in 1956 and remembers when mail was delivered twice a day and brigades of salesmen divided the city into territories, selling housewares and baked goods, milk, ice, vacuum cleaners, and Encyclopaedia Britannica, volumes A through Z, all door to door.

Now, it's down to one man in a battered '86 Pontiac, and he's got the whole city to himself.

"Just one horse pulling this wagon," says Clegg , who has a full head of white hair and a 6-foot frame slightly bent forward. "I may be the last of the Mohicans."

With his close shave, plaid shirt and striped tie, he's a walking anachronism, but so are some of the customers he's been calling on for 30 or 40 years. This particular afternoon, it's Amy Forbis, 78, whom he can usually count on to buy at least one Big D Blue brand toilet-bowl cleaner.

Forbis is back living in the house where she grew up on Olive Street, but she's moved many times in between, raised five children, buried one husband, remarried, and run a preschool and a knitting business.

Each time she moved, she would conclude she'd seen the last of Luther Clegg. Finally, here she is back in her childhood home, and Clegg is still making his rounds – sitting for long hours, recollecting names and streets and landmarks that everyone but he and his customers have forgotten. Col. Hobgood and Dr. Banner. Mr. Farley. Horse-drawn fire wagons. The old cigar factory, where his father opened the Clegg Hotel, on a section of old Walker Street so narrow that when his mother parked her 1925 Cadillac, Luther Clegg recalls, it blocked traffic.

By now, the grandfather clock in Amy Forbis' living room has chimed off a good hour and 15 minutes, all for the sale of two Big D Blue bowl cleaners, a $6.59 transaction Clegg records in detail in his leather receipt book.

The truth is, these door-to-door sales calls aren't the convenience they once were. He calls at odd hours and carries a limited line – carbon stainless steel scissors, Incredible brand spot remover – not much you couldn't pick up at the supermarket whenever you choose, maybe for less.

On the other hand, there is the matter of the light bulbs – regular 40- and 60-watt, candelabra style or floodlight – which are supposed to burn 5,000 hours, five times the life of bulbs sold in stores. It's something in the filament, Clegg says, and the brass threading that won't rust.

As for Clegg, the secret is anyone's guess. He gave up Camels when they hit 15 cents a pack, hasn't drunk coffee since he left the service, and makes sure to exercise the hip with the piece of titanium in it. He doesn't work Sundays, as a rule, but he never takes vacation – "unless that's what they give you with a shot in the arm." If he quit work, he's afraid he might wind up like the retired mill worker Mr. Farley told him about. After retiring, all the man did was watch TV. He was dead in six months.

So when the winter turns suddenly warm, the way it did last week, Clegg might park the Pontiac and walk through Fisher Park, remembering paths where as a boy he dug up worms for bait or the bandstand where the firemen gave Sunday concerts, played live on the radio.

He thinks about the two-story house on the corner where they moved when he was 8. It's condominiums now – Williamsburg on the Park – with no trace of the big porch and the stone steps where he first ventured out, selling the Saturday Evening Post for a nickel a copy.

It's all gone now. All that's left is the apple tree in one corner of the yard. And, of course, Luther Clegg.

– January 2, 2005

In the Turn Lane, Show Us a Sign

❄

Twelve dollars more.

All Sheila and Angela needed was $12 more to get a $38 room for the night, and with all these cars coming in and out of the SuperK, Home Depot and Circuit City, you wouldn't think it would take long.

Carrying hand-lettered signs saying, "DOWN ON MY LUCK" and "HOMELESS AND HUNGRY," they were the only ones working the intersection of Wendover and Bridford Parkway Wednesday afternoon.

With the way the wind gusted and the rain soaked through the women's cardboard signs, you'd think that even motorists who normally had doubts would today cave in, roll down the window and hold out a quarter or 50 cents.

But it was just the opposite.

Angela, 44, and Sheila, 34, had been working the intersection since late morning, and the weather was putting even more distance between them and the people in the cars.

"I've stood out here when it was so cold there were icicles hanging off me, and people wouldn't roll down their windows," Sheila said. "They look at you like, 'Why don't you get out of the rain?'"

Maybe part of this stone-faced response comes from stories people hear about some panhandler somewhere who lives in a condo, dresses up like a bum in the morning and takes in $200 a day.

"I'd like to know where that spot is," says Angela.

Maybe it's the competition at Wendover – too many people with signs and Bible verses printed in waterproof ink.

There's the self-described homeless cancer patient ("She does not have cancer," Sheila insists, "and she lives in the woods because she wants to.") There's the woman Angela says hogs the intersection with a neat little sign requesting "financial assistance." ("She's not even homeless," says Angela. "If I knew where to call, I'd report her.") And there's the guy who smells like booze and sleeps in a nearby junkyard – although he, the two women agree, at least is homeless.

Whatever the explanation, it's slow going out here, with Angela working the right-turn-only lane near Taco Bell, and Sheila standing on the Wendover median. The median is more risky, she admits, but at least you're on the driver's side.

Either way, most drivers pretend not to see them at all. A woman in a designer suit and an Isuzu Trooper cocks her head into a cell phone. A man in a silver Mercedes licks the end of an expensive-looking cigar.

Some stare at them like roadside attractions – a woman passenger eating an ice cream cone, a schoolgirl with a lapful of books. Two young guys in a red Z-28 pull up, and the passenger yells something out the window and laughs as they speed off.

"People holler things all the time," said Angela, who's wearing soiled jeans, two hooded jackets that are soaked through, and a tired expression. "They'll say, 'Get a job.' 'Get a life.' Something all of us want."

On and off for the past month or so, alternately seeing and trying not to see Angela and Sheila and their signs, I've wondered the same thing.

"Why don't you just get a job?"

Well, there's the long answer. Getting laid off, getting evicted, having your purse with your ID cards stolen, and trying to get a regular job when you don't have ID or a place to shower and sleep.

On days like this, when they can't find day labor jobs like construction site clean-up, all they have is a beat-up Mercury with no radio, no window crank on the driver's side and part of the front end missing. And they have this corner.

Sheila and Angela meet back at the Mercury to count their money.

"Twelve dollars," Angela says. "We need twelve more dollars."

The temperature is dropping and Sheila, who has a stomach virus, is becoming agitated at the prospect of sleeping in the car.

"I just wish the tables could turn for some of these people," she says. "They just ride right on. 'I got mine, you get yours.'"

"The only people who help you," says Angela, "are the ones who have been in your shoes. A lot of 'em are only one paycheck away from the same thing."

Lucky for me, I'm just here to observe. Unlike the people in the cars, I don't have to decide. Whether these two could find help within the system. Whether handing them a dollar is helping, or just a cheap way to feel charitable.

Or whether staring straight ahead and ignoring their cardboard signs is just blocking out a message I don't feel like reading, in between forays to Sam's Club and the La-Z-Boy Furniture Gallery.

It's not my problem, but I have to admit it. When I see a female driver hand Sheila a small bag of groceries, and a guy in a painter's van hold out a fluttering bill to Angela, I'm grateful.

The truth is, I'm ready to get back in my car and get into some dry things. I'm ready to go home.

— March 5, 1999

Once Upon a December Chill

❄

The snow came early that year, arriving the same morning in early December that Dona Bellamy answered a knock at the door and found the apartment manager waiting with a sheriff's deputy.

Bellamy, shivering in the doorway, showed them the papers from her doctor, saying that while she recovered from surgery, she could not perform her duties as a nurse's assistant at a retirement home. She had lost the job.

"We're sorry," the manager said. "We just have to evict you. At 1 o'clock, we'll be back to padlock the door."

So as the snow flew that morning in 2003, Bellamy's brother hastily rented a truck from U-Haul, and her five children, ages 7 to 16, told their mother not to cry and not to fuss. Just start packing.

Most of their things, they balled up into trash bags and took to a storage rental. The bare necessities, they took in suitcases to the home of a friend.

When the sheriff's deputy came back with the padlock, he started to apologize: I know it's a rough time ...

"I understand," Bellamy said.

The friend said they could stay as long as they needed. But making a gesture is one thing; being cooped up with five children over the long winter school break, quite another.

So as soon as Bellamy got her income tax refund in

January, she moved her children to a motel room at Knights Inn.

While she waited for her husband to be paroled on a 1988 robbery conviction, she got through that gray winter, one foot in front of the other.

She watched pennies, kept their groceries in a small fridge, cooked meals on a George Foreman grill, had their clothes organized in plastic bins.

She arranged for school buses to pick them up at the motel, where for the kids, the novelty had worn off.

And when at last Bellamy went back to working her 10-hour shifts, getting off at all hours, her big worry was her children getting off the bus with no one there to meet them.

"Don't worry, Mrs. Bellamy," the manager at the motel said. "I'll make sure the children get to your room."

Which he did. Every school day, he would call her at work to let her know they were home. Looking back on it, she can't fully explain why a stranger would do this for her – a manager at a budget motel, an immigrant from Pakistan or India, she guessed, with his own 24-hour business to run.

But it was the kind of small favor that helped the family survive until Bellamy could get back on her feet.

The school social worker at Hunter Elementary, where Bellamy's youngest were enrolled, collected money to pay the light bill after the mother's operation and made sure the family had food.

The pastor at Bellamy's church offered constant encouragement. Even the chaplain kept in touch from the prison where Bellamy's husband was nearing release.

And maybe after the year we had, a year of disasters

that exhausted the big reserves, these are the small things we don't hear about. The one-on-one favors cost a little money, sometimes no money, just the act of noticing when people are struggling. With no reserve, we're overwhelmed.

Which was the way Hunter School social worker Suzanne Fray felt, for a moment, when she answered the phone a year later, before Thanksgiving, and it was Dona Bellamy calling.

It's the social worker's bind – to help in emergencies, keeping the lights on and the sheriff at bay, hoping it won't be a family's way of life.

Fray took a deep breath and got ready to tell Bellamy that Hunter couldn't help her – the children had transferred to another school.

But Bellamy wasn't calling for help. She was back on her feet, able to do her nursing assistant's job again, and with the help of overtime from private duty, her income had gone from nothing to $35,000 a year.

Why was she calling? She'd bought several frozen turkeys, side dishes, desserts and snacks, and wanted to ask Fray where to deliver them.

Fray, surprised, stammered that Bellamy wasn't obligated to do that.

Bellamy insisted.

"I never forgot people who were there for me," she said. "You need a 'handout' sometimes. But it's not the end of the world."

– December 11, 2005

Santa's Coming,
on a Lighted Helicopter

❄

When the rotor on the light-up Santa Claus helicopter stopped turning a few years back over Holland Electric Co., drivers on U.S. 29 took it as a sign from above – or, from below, a half-staff salute to Bill Holland.

It was, in fact, a coincidence.

Holland, the late, legendary lineman whose crew used to hang the downtown Christmas decorations, acquired the copter in one of his rambling RV adventures. He loved it so much that he left it up all year, along with light-up tin soldiers, a nativity, a doctor's buggy, reindeer and a menagerie that outshone Noah's Ark in variety, not to mention kilowatt usage.

But wind and water took their toll, and everyone knows, if one light stops blinking, it breaks the whole circuit.

As Bill's son explained to the umpteenth Green's Supper Club regular calling to inquire about what was ailing the airborne landmark:

"It just quit working."

Not so for the Hollands, a three-generation clan of master electricians who could once drive up and down the back roads of Guilford County and point out which house, in which year, went from kerosene lanterns to pull cords and outlets under rural electrification in the '40s and '50s.

It's a dying breed: not the people, but the work. They wired this town, lit the ball fields from Revolution on, some two and three times, hung the stoplights, built the circuits and flipped on the pumps at Lake Townsend, as the trout tried to wriggle free.

Above all, they built substations. That's where a Duke Power stops and a Cone Mills or a Burlington Industries starts – dangerous, high-voltage work at the transformers, pulling wire as big around as your arm.

Bill and his wife, Dot, like both their fathers before them, were electricians, as were their brothers, their children, and in a few cases, their children's children. No job too big.

And no job, evidently, too small. If only Dot Holland could find out which one of these lights is malfunctioning on the Santa helicopter, brought back here years ago from a camping trip in Pigeon Forge, Tenn.

It began with the kind of phone call that made Holland's son, Billy, shudder, more than any ice storm outage or hurricane. It was Bill Holland on vacation. Bill at the auction, Bill at the flea market. There was no telling.

For example, "Get up here to Asheville and bring all the trucks," one such dispatch from Bill had begun. Bill had found the deal of a lifetime: a surplus of Winnebago-size seat belts, 34,000 of them, priced to sell at 11 1/2 cents apiece.

"I've never been so mad at my father in my life. We really went at it that time," his son recalls. "Where's the PROFIT margin in that?"

So maybe after 34,000 Winnebago seat belts, one

more phone call from the Smokies over Labor Day weekend from some potpourri-smelling year-round Christmas
shop would be, in comparison, a cake-walk.

Holland had made a rare find – for all he knew, one
of a kind.

"Drive on up to Pigeon Forge, and bring the trailer,"
Bill said. "I found a Santa Claus helicopter , and it won't
fit in the RV."

❄ ❄ ❄

In the fluorescent-lit back room of Holland Electric
Co., the stories fly from one creaky swivel chair to the
next on a dreary winter's eve.

Yet by some sleight of hand, work and play have
swapped places, like two schoolboys trading seats when
the teacher has her back turned.

The Hollands keep scrapbooks and photo albums of
jobs that were showcases – McMichael High School in
Stoneville – or jobs like Hurricane Camille that linger in
dreams, and not with visions of sugar plums. They take
them out and pore over them, the way the next family
might pass around snapshots of a trip to Disney.

Vacations, on the other hand, are mostly filed by
mishap.

"Tell about the time in Daytona when Ann held the
flashlight and fell in the ditch," Dot instructs Billy, then
gives a sideways wink. "It's OK to put that in. She lives
in Kernersville and doesn't take the paper. She'll never
know the difference."

Likewise, in the front shop of Holland Electric, work
and play trade places, but in the opposite way.

The walls are covered with license plates of states the

family visited, with banners from every state fair Dot and Bill ever attended back to 1950 and kitschy attractions – Frontier Days, Buffalo Bill's Museum, Land of Oz Beech Mountain, Ripley's Believe It or Not.

But for Billy's money, you could keep your tacky Wild West shows, you could believe it or not.

That's because the week of Aug. 19, 1969, he saw the whole thing from his father's bucket truck in Nelson County, Va. – an event the National Weather Service wildly underestimated as a "residual storm" of a Category 5 cyclone named Camille out of the Gulf – bringing an 8-foot crest of water, enough to knock out every bridge, kill 259 people and drown the birds in the trees.

Billy, 13, would be home in time for the first day of school. But in Holland fashion, he would work the bucket truck during the worst flash flood in Appalachian history.

❄ ❄ ❄

The Holiday Inn was the only place in the whole valley that was serving food, and by this time they were starving.

As they waited for breakfast, they went ahead and ordered lunch to go. An exhausted Bill Holland watched his 13-year-old son like a hawk from across the linen and silverware, willing him to mind his manners in front of the big-shot joining the linemen at the table, the head of Southern Railway.

There had been only one road into Virginia – U.S. 29 – and only one lane that wasn't washed out. A state trooper walked in front of the Hollands' lead truck, inch by inch, to make sure the wheel didn't go off the pavement and into the rushing, muddy river.

The trooper would put his boot down and nod back at the driver, Billy's uncle, Tommy Rumley. The first thing they noticed was a two-story farmhouse that had washed down the mountainside, sitting in the road. The second thing, cows, 30 or 40 feet up in the trees.

The Hollands' job was to light the river, so that Southern Railway could rebuild, and the work could go on 24 hours. Billy's job? To go up and down a slope on a pulley and a rope. He kept stepping on a car roof buried in mud. Finally, a rescuer realized that inside the car was a girl and her mother, three days dead, the woman's hands still clutching the steering wheel.

The rescuer had a heart attack and died. Billy kept working, a whole week, until it was time to go home for school. Or maybe his father and his uncles had just had enough of cows in trees, and bodies being helicoptered in to a morgue the Amish set up on a main road.

The Hollands were told to drive to Lovingston. There, like depleted troops giving their ammo to incoming replacements, they were to give all their tools and poles to the crews coming in, and send the railway a bill. Which leads us back to the linen table at the Holiday Inn, where the president of Southern Railway was picking up the tab.

Billy, unable to wait another moment for something to eat, plucked a pack of Saltines and a pat of butter from the middle of the table and made himself a sandwich, as Bill Holland watched, simmering with disapproval.

The next to reach for the butter and crackers was Uncle Tommy. And finally, Mr. Southern Railway Big Shot himself.

Billy smiled across the linen table at his stewing father. He had upended Bill Holland. This once.

❋ ❋ ❋

Eleven and a half cents apiece. "Where's the profit margin in THAT?" Bill Holland would feed his words back to him. How. Many. Times.

Yes, 34,000 Winnebago seat belts turned out to be a gold mine. Every time Bill made a run west, he would take a box, and each belt fetched $5 or $6 apiece. That's what? 21,000 percent profit? Times 34,000?

"What he did," Billy says in defeat, "was rub my nose in it."

One thing led to another. Bill walked into an RV manufacturing plant that was closing in the Midwest, was asked what he would pay for the contents, jotted a few numbers down, and the man laughed. Bill started to walk away.

"Whoa," the owner protested. "We're not done talking."

Bill was in the RV business now, and did well, as usual, for years. Just had the knack. He didn't live to see the rest of it go away – Cone, and then the Burlington Industries they helped build on Friendly to make room for something grand, or grander or grandest.

Who can keep track anymore?

But somewhere up the line, he gets the last laugh anyway. Dot, giving up on that Made-in-Taiwan helicopter, was on her way to Banner Elk the other week when something made her stop at a no-name roadside stand on 421. It turned out Bill's Pigeon Forge find hadn't been one-of-a-kind after all.

Last week, on a dreary winter's day, passers-by on U.S. 29 beheld, for the first time in years, a fully functional Santa helicopter above Holland Electric Co.

It felt like Christmas morning, like finding 34,000 Winnebago seat belts for 11 and a half cents apiece.

It was the deal of a lifetime.

— December 21, 2008

PART 3

Cold War Stories

A Silent Night:
Christmas in the Ardennes

✳

They were about a week into the winter Battle of the Bulge, which would turn out to be Hitler's last western offensive before Germany surrendered the following spring. The trouble was, the men of B Company's 307th Airborne Combat Engineers didn't know that yet.

No, all they knew was that the trucks brought them to Belgium and dropped them off in the snow in the middle of the night with plenty of ammunition, but no food, no overcoats, nothing but the same cotton uniforms with the 82nd "All American" patch they'd worn since they jumped into Holland back in September 1944.

Now, it was the depths of December in the Ardennes Forest, the ground too hard to dig foxholes. The valley where they stopped was black and silent, except for the Germans taunting them from a hill, saying they would come and kill them while they slept.

The next thing my dad's sergeant knew, an old Belgian was poking him awake with a stick, saying, *Come in the house. Get warm.* So they followed him to a farmhouse built on top of a barn. Inside the barn, this wave hit them – the body heat of the cows – and the men started running around, laying their hands on the cows.

"The cows didn't like that," the sergeant, Walter Kearns, was telling me the other day, from his home in New Jersey. "But it's amazing what a little warmth will do when you've been that cold for that long."

At 26, he would have been the old man of the outfit in December 1944. Today, at age 84, he's the only one left to tell the story.

It's a story that always eluded my family at Christmas, though we were aware of it hanging overhead, like mistletoe. We would set up our little manger with the real straw and the frosted blue light bulb, put on Nat King Cole, and it would happen every year – my dad would get quiet, far off. Later, he'd cheer up, when my uncles got there, or if Kearns called from New Jersey.

In Europe for 3 years during World War II, they were best friends. During the devastating Operation Market Garden depicted in "A Bridge Too Far," they slept in a pup tent for a month near Nijmegen, where they saved the bridge over the Waal River, but lost much of their unit doing it.

For R&R, they were sent to Rheims, camping out and living on fruitcakes. Unfortunately, this put the 307th less than a day's drive from where SS tanks were about to break through and put a "bulge" in the western front.

So now, they didn't even have fruitcakes. If they were lucky, they would find an abandoned car for shelter. If not, they'd huddle, eight or nine men, to keep from freezing.

"If you were in the middle, you would actually get too hot," Kearns was saying. "The guys on the outside would be half warm and half cold."

Hearing only bits and pieces over the years, I never knew which scene my father replayed in his head, while we put tinsel on the tree and Johnny Mathis sang "Winter Wonderland." I knew, for one thing, that a soldier died in his arms, alternately calling out for his mother and for the only one there to help him, my dad.

And on Christmas Eve, sleeping in yet another barn, my father became so miserable when a green replacement sang "Silent Night" that he threatened him with a silent eternity if he didn't shut up.

By Jan. 4, plenty of them did meet eternity, or at least the SS. My dad survived, by an eighth of an inch: He was running and holding onto his helmet when an SS bullet went through his hand, just missing his temple. A Jeep took him to the hospital in the falling snow, so covered up the nurses nicknamed him "Snowman."

After that, he wrote his girlfriend, my mom, that he wanted to marry her. But first, he wanted to get back to his unit, which before it was over would cross the Rhine, stumble upon two Nazi death camps, and finally sleep in a 24-room mansion on Berlin's Mozartstrasse – about as far as they could get from a pup tent.

That spring in a bombed-out Berlin, they finally had all the cognac and beer they wanted, but of the original 15 men in the unit, there were only three left to enjoy it. So there would always be something missing, something that diluted the comfort and joy.

And that was why, during the fighting, none of them would ever accept a weekend pass to Paris or the Riviera when the officers were trying to raise morale. As much as they all missed home, being away from the front didn't feel right, either.

The only pass Sgt. Kearns remembers was to visit the hospital in England where they'd transferred my dad, whom Kearns assumed was going home after he recovered.

"I never expected to see him again," Kearns was saying the other day. "What made you so nutty – and what made your father come back (to the fight) – was that nobody wanted to leave the outfit. He didn't have to come back. He could have gone home and forgotten the war."

So I don't know. It could be that all these Christmases past, he just missed the buddies he'd huddled with in the snow of the Ardennes, to keep from freezing to death. Maybe he started to feel like the one on the outside of the huddle – half warm, half cold.

And now, of the three who got to Berlin, it's just Kearns. He still sends my mom a Christmas card.

"I hope Guy (Ahearn) is scouting around up there (or maybe down below?)" he wrote this year. "Anyhow, 'The Band of Brothers' will be getting together soon."

– December 25, 2002

Bethlehem Calling:
Refugee from the "City of Christ"

❄

It was the one thing her grandfather took with him from their village in Palestine – an iron skeleton key, heavy, brown with age, a family heirloom with no practical use anymore.

The key is to a deserted house, in a village wiped out by columns of tanks and missile attacks, one of those pastoral, biblical places erased from the rutted map of the West Bank.

Israeli troops occupying these places in the wilderness outside Bethlehem, pushing east toward the Dead Sea, planted clumps of cactus at the approaches to the ruins. That's one way to locate where the villages used to be.

And at age 19, Manar Majed Faraj may never live in the home to which the key belongs. A third-generation refugee, she was born in the holy city of Bethlehem, in the Dheisa camp for Palestinians, 12,000 crowded into a quarter of a square mile.

"The houses in the camp are on top of each other," the GTCC exchange student was saying last week. "If you open your window, you don't see trees, you don't see sky. Just the faces of your neighbors."

Finished with exams, she was sitting in the living room of a Greensboro friend, near a bay window looking out on Lake Daniel Park. The pretty, dark-eyed student, an accomplished dancer who hopes to be a journalist one day, was remembering her first trip to America in 1999.

"The first thing I noticed was a playground. All these huge playgrounds and toys," she said. "I was 13 or 14 years old. All I wanted to do was play, like I was in kindergarten."

In the camp where she grew up, there are no playgrounds, no toys. Children play with shell casings they find in the dirt alleys and go to schools with 60 students to a class.

Particularly since the uprising in 2000, nothing is normal, except military checkpoints, night patrols, the scream of helicopter missiles.

And increasingly, the 4,000-year-old "city of Christ" is surrounded by high concrete walls and electric fences, with only two gates in and out.

Tourists who once flocked to Manger Square and the Church of the Nativity, built on the spot believed to be Jesus' birthplace, have all but stopped coming. Souvenir stands that sold little mangers carved from olive wood closed. There is an exodus of Palestinian Christians – descended from the first followers of Christ.

Desperate to save the city, Bethlehem's mayor last month traveled to Washington, declaring Bethlehem an "open city" issuing its own passport, inviting the faithful to visit.

But to Manar, the city with an ancient reputation for hospitality, a city lit up each December, fragrant with pine and incense, is now a forbidding place. When she phones home to her siblings, they talk about which friends have been arrested, which are wanted. They talk of the wall, so high they can't see the sun rise and set.

Even an ocean away, she sits on the edge of her seat, never at ease, never at home, except in a crowded camp with a tale of tragedy behind every door. Hers is the tale of her grandfather, who ventured out to get food during a 24-hour curfew, doubting an old man could pose a threat. He never came back and was shot to death.

As Manar searches for the right words, her eyes grow wide with fear, and sadness. And something else grows there, too – but not hard and spiny, like the cactus in the ruins.

What grows is hope. It's Bethlehem calling her, and when she finishes her education, she'll return. Her father inherited the iron key. Manar, the oldest of six, will inherit it next.

"The key is the hope that I won't stay a refugee," she said. "My key is my hope to go home someday."

– December 25, 2005

Pebbles from a "Kindertransport"

❄

Nelly Falk may be the only person to perish in Auschwitz who has a tombstone in Greensboro. No remains. Just a stone, showing someone was here and remembered.

That person is her son, Walter. And in contrast to his mother's desolate fate, the tale of how he was spared the same demise is one dim shaft of daylight that penetrated, briefly, the black vault of the Holocaust.

His is the forgotten interlude of the "Kindertransports," which delivered Walter Falk and 10,000 other Jewish children from the jaws of Nazi Germany to England.

Like the dark chocolates he arranges on a china plate for his afternoon coffee, Falk's memories are bittersweet.

On one hand, he can't escape the fact that his mother, a small, careful woman who could not bear to leave her elderly parents in Germany, was meanwhile taken on a cattle car to the death camp in Poland in September 1942 and herded into a gas chamber – one of 6 million to die, including 1.5 million children.

On the other hand, the paradox: Before the curtain of night fell on Germany, strangers swooped in and snatched these 10,000 to safety. Which is how Falk lived to be an old man, to pour his coffee and tell the tale in the quiet of his Greensboro kitchen.

"It's an unanswered question," he begins, in his still-thick Black Forest accent. "Some people say, 'The good Lord wanted it that way.' Other people would say, 'Where was the good Lord when they killed all those people?' All my life, bad things happened around me. And still, here I am."

❅ ❅ ❅

"Bad things," to be sure, didn't begin with Kristallnacht, the 1938 pogrom in which Jewish men were rounded up in cities across Germany, synagogues were burned and so many Jewish shops' windows were smashed that it was literally called "crystal night," the night of the broken glass.

No, even in the city of Karlsruhe, where 11-year-old Walter Falk lived with his widowed mother, the storm of mob violence was approaching.

Already, they'd been evicted from their lovely, terraced apartment because a Nazi Party member moved in next door. Falk was sent to a segregated school for Jewish children, on the grounds of an insane asylum.

Yet until Kristallnacht, the well-to-do Jews who went back centuries in Germany engendered hope that it wouldn't last, that it might blow over. That fragile illusion shattered like glass on Nov. 9, 1938.

Falk's makeshift school had dismissed early, and he returned home to find the picture windows of the Jewish shoe store downstairs broken, new shoes strewn about the street.

Upstairs, his mother was crying. Nazis had raided the home, pulled curtains and paintings off the walls, looking for a safe. Finding nothing, they left. Clearly, they would be back.

Some were lucky. Falk's uncle, a "nogoodnik" who played cards with police friends, was tipped off to buy a train ticket to Basel, Switzerland, and return safely the next day. Another of Falk's adult male relatives wasn't lucky. He was taken to Dachau, the concentration camp near Munich.

"He must have said something wrong," Falk said. "He came home in a cigar box."

Falk and his mother left for his grandparents' country village, where it was calm, for now. But immediately, Falk's mother set about finding the boy a way out of Germany – to Shanghai, Buenos Aires, no matter.

He also applied for an exit visa to Palestine – a route the Nazi regime actually encouraged before the war. Palestine had been carved into the British Mandate after World War I, and sending Jews there was a way for Germany to antagonize England.

But through a friend, Falk's mother learned of the Kindertransports, which had been put through British Parliament with the blessing of Neville Chamberlain, the prime minister better known for a historic blunder.

To appease Adolf Hitler and avert a new world war, Chamberlain left the Munich Conference with a "nonaggression pact" with Germany, a worthless piece of paper when Germany invaded Poland a year later.

But it was in that window between Kristallnacht and the march into Poland on Sept. 1, 1939, that Falk boarded one of the trains that traveled through Holland to a ferry across the English Channel.

An estimated 10,000 Jewish youths were sheltered in England for the duration of the war. Some lived with adopted families; others, like Falk, lived in a series of hostels, farms and homes for children, such as Lord Balfour's estate in Scotland.

In the United States, there had also been a Children's

Rescue Bill introduced in Congress to provide a temporary safe haven for Jewish children 14 and under, but the bill never got out of committee.

Despite an outpouring from the American public of offers to shelter children, a coalition of immigration opponents lobbied against the effort. Publicly, they testified that the rescue bill would cause the country to be "flooded with foreigners" and people "who could never be loyal to the United States."

Privately, however, opposition to the rescue bill wasn't strictly out of fear that the children would endanger the country. In his diary, now housed in the National Archives, a highly placed State Department diplomat, J. Pierrepont Moffat, recalled a conversation at a cocktail party for the Washington elite.

"The problem with the (child rescue) bill," Moffat quoted the wife of then-U.S. Commissioner of Immigration James Hougheling as saying, "was that 20,000 children would all too soon grow up into 20,000 ugly adults."

As for Walter Falk, who had kissed his mother goodbye and boarded a train out of Germany, thinking they would be reunited soon, the outbreak of war in 1939 erased any chance that his mother would safely exit Germany.

Yet even while German air raids in the Battle of Britain darkened the English sky, Falk managed to correspond with his mother via a Swiss relative. Nelly Falk's letters were careful, guarded.

One day, they stopped coming.

❄ ❄ ❄

From out in the bare December garden, he chooses the smoothest stones, the ones with the rough edges worn away by weather or by time. He washes them in the kitchen sink, then puts them in his pocket on the way to the cemetery.

In August, his wife, Ginger, died – like Falk, she was a German Jew who managed to escape the war, fleeing to Argentina. They met in New York City, where he immigrated after the war to be with an aunt.

He never set foot in Germany again until 1950, by then a private in Uncle Sam's Army, on a weekend pass. It was too soon to process it all, so he settled for being uppity with the Germans, he and a buddy parking their combat boots on the facing seats in the train compartment.

"Verboten!" the conductor huffed.

"Hah?" they jeered back, cupping their hands behind their ears. "We don't understand German!"

Out of the Army, he became a salesman, moved south, had a good life with Ginger all these years – "on borrowed time," he likes to say.

Now, he's alone with his cat and his papers and his china coffee cups. He still gets visits from Ginger's home nurse, a Muslim woman who escaped her own set of horrors in Africa's Sierra Leone – exiting via England, just like Walter Falk.

On a December afternoon, Isha Conteh accompanies the old man to the Jewish cemetery near Four Seasons. Falk puts on his black skull cap, and holding the smooth, cold stones in his palm, he places one on top of his wife's polished-granite headstone and one on top of his mother's.

It's the Jewish way. Just a stone, to show those who come later that someone was here, and remembered.

– December 10, 2006

The Last Medal:
An Old Soldier's Young Ghosts

❄

Until the night an Army doctor was locking up the morgue and heard something move in the corner, everybody thought James A. Garner was dead.

First were the soldiers who carried him off the hill in North Korea, his leg blown off by a Chinese mortar shell and an impossible hole in his chest where shrapnel cut through his armored vest.

The medic gave him a second shot of morphine – he wasn't supposed to, but he figured Garner was going to die anyway. Even Garner's mother had already gotten word back in Winston, coming to the door to find two stone-faced officers from Fort Bragg standing on her front porch.

So 48 years ago, that's how Garner's story nearly ended. He was 19 – just out of high school and basic training – tossed in with a pile of dead soldiers at the evac hospital, and left in a dark, freezing-cold morgue the GIs called "the dog pound."

Officially deceased. That is, until this doctor flips the lights back on, finds where the sound is coming from, and realizes that Garner and another soldier are still alive.

Of the two, only Garner survived. And it happened that way over and over, like some unseen hand picking

him out, and lately that's keeping him up at night. Faces
crowd before him after all these years, just now, when
he's finally about to get his due.

You see, Garner is getting a medal – The Soldier's
Medal – for having risked his life during the Korean War to
save two soldiers from drowning in the Kumnwha River.

He pulled one out and laid him on the river bank,
then looked back and saw the second man disappear
below the surface. Too late, it seemed, but something
made Garner jump in anyway – and the churn of the
water happened to spin the man back around so that
Garner could save him.

Then just last year, a retired lieutenant colonel living
in Kernersville hears the story from a friend, decides
Garner deserves some recognition, and starts doing
research to get the medal approved.

But you know the thing about digging through these
long-ago incident reports? Or looking up half-forgotten
names in out-of-town phone books? After 48 years, you
never know quite what you'll stir up.

It's even true for a lucky guy like Garner. Nice wife,
nice job with the parks department, nice house over by
Reynolds Park Golf Course – a course he helped inte-
grate, where they named a rec center after him because
of his charity golf tournaments and his work with
amputees.

He shows me down to the den, where a flag and a
Purple Heart are in a frame on the wall, with a picture
of a young soldier in uniform, one trouser leg empty, sitting on his mother's porch with his dog.

They were all young guys in "A" Company – 18 when
they got their draft notices – dropped into combat with
no time to adjust, no one to show them around.

They'd been down in the trenches for a couple of weeks, sleeping on the ground, cold to the bone, when he and two buddies decided to eat their dinner above ground for a change. You can guess what happened next – pow, pow, pow – a sniper picked off the friend on one side of Garner, and the one on the other side.

Garner dove for cover, and later saw that one of the friends took two bullets in the face. One of those bullets was meant for you, a medic told Garner.

Still, that's not the worst. There was a fellow soldier who was his childhood playmate, his old schoolmate who joined up at the same time as Garner – hit by a mortar and blown to bits, and Garner picking up the parts and putting them back together. Because that was his friend.

But I guess the clincher comes just a few months back, when the research for the medal turns up something else. In the months after Garner was wounded, and lay in a coma in an Army hospital, "A" Company was overrun and decimated not far from the hill where Garner was hit. Of more than 100 men, only 14 survived.

So if he hadn't been wounded and left for dead, he probably wouldn't have lived. And there would be no James A. Garner Jr., and no James A. Garner III, who is 8 months old and tearing around upstairs in a walker as his grandfather tells the story.

They'll all be proud when a congressman pins the medal on Garner at the courthouse a few weeks from now, and Garner will be proud, too. But the way he sees it, he's been wearing that medal all these years. And it weighs heavily.

– March 26, 2000

A Daughter Who Perished in the War Without End

❄

You have to understand about sailors, her father was saying. After 22 years in the Navy, he would know.

They don't think about the danger in these six-month deployments, when the only contact with home is letters that take weeks to arrive, and maybe some static-laced phone calls patched through the satellite system on a ship like the USS Cole.

"They think about the fun and the adventure of seeing the world," Ronald Francis was saying. "Taking pictures. Buying artifacts in these exotic ports. Then coming home and swapping sea stories. Sailors don't think about not coming back."

But when they learned a week ago that Lakeina Francis, 19, wasn't coming back, her first letter hadn't yet found its way to her family's mailbox on a twisting rural road south of Statesville.

She'd only been gone two weeks. They weren't even sure she was on the Cole, until the night a Navy chaplain and a couple of grave looking sheriff's deputies were suddenly standing in the porch light.

So soon, it seemed unthinkable. Basic training at Great Lakes, specialized A-School in San Antonio, a final leave home in September, then her mother Sandra was driving her to Norfolk to report for duty.

Lakeina joked at the last minute – *No, put me in the trunk! I don't want to go!* Then shrugged it off: *Nah, I'm a sailor.* A moment's hesitation, her mother wonders?

But her father had no doubt she was ready. Not after she did enough push-ups to outpace her younger brother, a football standout at West Rowan High. Not to mention her graduating second in her class from basic training, the same boot camp her father went through 22 years earlier.

He's a practical, realistic man, Ronald Francis, and he gave her advice: Stay focused on getting an education. Try to make rank soon, the retired chief petty officer advised, rank has its privileges.

Sure enough, she'd made master sergeant and was just shy of an E-4. *Boy, if I keep this up,* she'd told her grandmother in a phone call, *I'll be up there with Dad.*

Lakeina elected to be a mess officer. This surprised them all, since she hated to cook. But once she shipped out, her father began to see the logic.

For one thing, she could phone home often, seemingly at will. Perks like that come with being a cook, he explained – pleased, impressed that she was already negotiating the tight quarters of a warship.

But sitting in his living room Friday afternoon, going over the whole thing with one more reporter, it was happening too fast for Ronald Francis. The budding pride over the girl in dress blues – a portrait taken just this summer – next to a stack of local papers with headlines that go from "missing" to "presumed dead."

In his raw, wrung-out fever of grief, the enormity hasn't set in. But with this last phone call from the Navy, he knows it will. A week after a suicide bombing tore the

Cole's hull apart as Lakeina was setting up for dinner, investigators found her body.

The parents couldn't help holding out for a miracle, even after seeing the massive hole in the ship. They just never felt that terrible premonition people say you're supposed to feel when a child dies. And after all, hadn't an earthquake victim survived 12 days in the rubble in Mexico City?

Nevertheless, the week's headlines rolled along like a drumbeat of inevitability. Friday, Lakeina's remains arrived in Dover, and Saturday they were en route to Salisbury, where the family will identify them just to be sure. But that task won't fall to her mother, an outwardly serene woman, and Lakeina's grandmother also refused. Not wanting that sight before her for the rest of her days.

So it falls to Ronald Francis – the first one who saw her at birth, who taught her to swim when she was still a baby, and taught her dance. She used to stand on top of my shoes, he remembers, holding his empty palms out, imagining his only daughter grasping his hands for balance.

One day soon, I guess they'll walk out to the mailbox on the country road and the letter their daughter mailed from the Cole will be there. And the six rolls of undeveloped film that were in Lakeina's locker on the ship – her grandmother was planning to have them processed, maybe finish the scrapbook from basic training.

But when Lakeina Francis comes home this weekend, there will be no sea stories to swap.

– October 22, 2000

Sergeant Shinn Takes a Holiday

❄

I n the car on the way home from the airport, he had the peculiar sensation of being vulnerable. Peculiar when you consider that, other than these past two weeks of leave in Greensboro, he spent most of 2003 in Baghdad.

So here he is riding along 68, no Kevlar helmet, no body armor, no Humvee. Not to mention, no M-16. From the corner of his eye, he sees a car driving too fast, coming too close. He feels his body tense, and reminds himself: You're here. You're not there.

Sgt. Jason Shinn, 29, came home for the holidays, one of the few members of the Greensboro-based 422nd Civil Affairs Battalion to be granted leave after 10 months in Iraq. They were among the first units to cross the border from Kuwait with the 3rd Infantry Division and fight their way north to Baghdad last March.

Now, the 3rd Infantry is long gone, and Shinn's unit, mostly reservists like himself, are in a holding pattern, policing an occupied city. It's a curious limbo – part kicking in doors, part handing out candy and soccer balls. Now that the more substantive tasks of getting schools up and running, establishing trash pickup or building parks are complete, Shinn's team has just one mission. Not to get shot.

So they go talk to residents they've talked to a thousand times. They write daily reports that somebody up the chain of command supposedly reads. They watch DVDs. They talk about what they'll do when they get home.

Yet it turns out that home is in limbo as well. There's the house in Julian he has never lived in – he and his wife, Kim, were still having it built when he was called up last January. His job managing a Ramada Inn hasn't been filled, but it's costing the company, he knows. And he won't finish his college degree — not this year anyway.

But he tries to enjoy his two weeks home. Going for a walk without having to carry 10 pounds of ammo. Seeing people flock to after-Christmas sales, or watching them tee off on the golf course, not a care in the world.

Now and then, he turns on the news, and it's one of two story lines he knows by heart: "It's either 'We soldiers are glad to serve and George Bush is God,' or it's 'The war is bad and here's today's body count.' And neither one is true."

The truth is, he has seen stupidity and nobility and kindness and atrocity. Old women running up to him in the streets, handing him bread and tea. Roads lined with corpses, stray dogs feeding off them. And every time you turn around, somebody's working on a book. The guy from CNN with the bodyguard. The previous battalion commander, who got shot at, once.

Shinn feels like two people sometimes. There's the person he is here, and the person over there, playing the soldier. Just as he's getting used to the scene change, it's time to go back.

A couple of nights before he leaves, they go to eat at Outback. The place is packed, noisy, confusing. Kim looks down and sees that he's holding one of the big steak knives like a weapon, the way you hold a survival knife. He's not even conscious of it, and that scares his wife. On the other hand, she knows, if he loses that survival instinct for the sake of two weeks' leave, that will scare her more.

Because either way, Sgt. Jason Shinn is catching a flight out of Baltimore tonight, and sometime Monday, he'll be in a Humvee headed back to Baghdad, holding an M-16 and watching from the corner of his eye for any sudden moves.

— December 28, 2003

The Scout Who Went to War

❄

The last time they locked eyes was before his son's second tour of Iraq.

They were both in Greensboro – Andrew getting ready to rejoin the Marines in his Mobile Assault unit, his father, Roland Russoli Sr., about to leave for mission work in the mountains of Mongolia, between Russia and China.

When it was time for Russoli to go through airport security, he turned to say goodbye. What Andrew said would later come back to haunt him.

"He said, 'Watch your back,'" the father recalled. "It was a strange look. Like he wouldn't see me again."

Russoli came home to Greensboro last week, visiting for the first time since Andrew's funeral in November 2005. A few months after that cryptic goodbye at PTI airport, Andrew was killed by a roadside bomb in Iraq, the first soldier from Greensboro to die in the war, but not the last.

Sipping coffee last week in a booth at Tex & Shirley's, Russoli could see across the parking lot the Macaroni Grill where they had dinner together that summer, between the son's first and second tour.

Andrew was quiet that night, different. Early in his first tour of Iraq, he had been full of boyish bravado. In one letter, he described how a bomb blew up in front of their vehicle, creating a massive cloud of sand and dust, from which the Humvee emerged unscathed on the other side.

"It was just like the part in 'The Man in the Iron Mask,' " Andrew wrote. "It was so cool."

But by the time he came back that summer before his second tour, he didn't want to watch movies anymore, especially his favorite, "Black Hawk Down," about a 1993 Mogadishu helicopter assault.

No, there had been too much reality in between. He had been through 19 firefights, had been wounded and received a Purple Heart, and in summer 2005, he was nevertheless home in one piece. On the outside, anyway.

Inside, the father wasn't sure. He looked into Andrew's green eyes and remembered a boy, full of fun, who always hooked a finger in his father's pocket when they crossed the street. How was that boy doing with all this?

"He was having nightmares about some of the things that occurred, about shooting people and watching them die," Russoli said . "He was in battles. It's hard to do that and still be that little boy inside. It takes a big piece of you."

The night at Macaroni Grill, Russoli's older son had left the table when Andrew finally spoke, talking about what he wanted to do after his second tour of Iraq.

"I think I want to become a firefighter," he told his father. "I want to save lives."

❄ ❄ ❄

It gets so cold in Ulaanbaatar that it burns, as if you were holding a Bic lighter too close to your cheek. It was 27 below the morning Russoli left 10 days ago on his 32-hour trek home from the city between four mountains.

From Greensboro, where Andrew graduated from Northwest and where his father directed volunteers for Habitat for Humanity, Ulaanbaatar is the edge of the world.

And no better place to be, when a whole piece of the future has been erased – all the birthdays, holidays, snapshots never to be. How do you get through the motions? That was the question the father of another Northwest graduate since killed in Iraq asked Russoli, a more experienced member of this unenviable fraternity.

How do you do Christmas?

"You can't do things the same way," Russoli answered. "It's too painful."

After returning to Mongolia from his son's funeral – around the same time President Bush visited the country and met privately with Russoli – the father found a way to do things differently.

He canceled the morning English classes he teaches in Ulaanbaatar and went to work in an orphanage run by French nuns.

The children there have been abandoned – some left as toddlers on street corners, some dumped in trash cans as babies, this in a city where homeless adults routinely freeze to death.

So last Christmas, Russoli and his wife, Sarah, a Peace Corps medical officer he married two years back, spent $100 on black market toys – a mountain of puzzles, dolls, Lincoln Logs and trucks.

Russoli put on the orphanage's heavy wool Santa suit, with a cheap beard that slipped to and fro, and watched each face, as the children carried off their piles of treasure.

They taught him something, as he sat there sweating

in his Santa suit and his cheap beard. In an orphanage on the frozen edge of the world, children abandoned on street corners and left in garbage cans could still be alive in this moment and still feel joy, not dwelling on the past.

They took his mind off a man he will never get to know, a handsome little boy who hooked a finger in his father's pocket as they crossed the street together. A boy he can't let go.

— December 17, 2006

En Route to Iraq, the Boy Who Fought Fires

❄

On the gray Friday after Thanksgiving, 24 hours before standing in formation in the Fort Bragg rain with his 82nd Airborne company bound for Iraq, Pfc. Clay Hartsook dangled his cowhide boots from the counter of the firehouse kitchen and took a last look around.

Other than his mother's house in "The Ridge," this is the only place Hartsook, 22, ever called home. A junior firefighter in training at 15, he went on his first fire call at 18, and became a volunteer fireman in exchange for room and board at Station 51, across from Northwest High in Oak Ridge.

Since the war started, three of his Northwest classmates have been killed in Iraq: his friends Andrew Russoli and Adam Lucas, and Nicholas Gibbs, who he didn't know as well.

With that said, and with Hartsook's pregnant wife spending the few dwindling hours left with him in the big TV room at the firehouse, why volunteer for the Army? And why the 82nd?

Hartsook has three reasons, spelled out clearly as a 911 call piped through the firehouse speakers in the phonetic alphabet of an emergency dispatch.

Andrew. Adam. Nicholas.

❄ ❄ ❄

Some fires, in the end, must be left to burn. The 96-year-old house on Haw River Road was such a fire.

The fine, hand-built wooden home was one of those disappearing throwbacks to an Oak Ridge that predated subdivisions and highway cloverleafs, and even predated the Oak Ridge Fire Department itself.

In 1954, after too many houses and general stores burned down here in the sticks, a group of businessmen, farmers and textile workers banded together to form the volunteer fire company, passing the hat to buy a '53 Chevrolet truck, which a local welder worked late nights to convert.

But there was a joke about volunteer RFDs of the era, an era in which Clay Hartsook's grandfathers on both sides were volunteer firemen. The joke contained a kernel of truth: "Save the chimneys!" the motto went.

"The population was so sparse that fires didn't get called in until they were fully involved," recalls Oak Ridge Fire Chief Bill Newman, whose father, was a founding member. "So by the time you got there, about all that was left was the chimneys."

Now, the house on Haw River Road was a whole different ball game, a different century in fire fighting.

This was, after all, 2006. Firefighters today wear oxygen bottles and go to school for 18 months to be certified as EMTs. Gone are the days of jumping on the fire truck's tailboard and hanging on for dear life – thanks to OSHA – a memory almost as distant as bucket brigades and trampolines used to catch survivors leaping from upstairs windows.

In hindsight, however, Hartsook, his Uncle Steve

Simmons and the other firefighters of Stations 51 and 15 could have used a trampoline on the gusty February night when they were the first engine companies at the six-alarm fire on Haw River Road.

The house was billowing smoke, engulfed in flames by the time the firefighters went in, put the first-floor blaze out and climbed the stairs to the second floor. Inexplicably, the first floor then reignited with a roar, trapping two teams of firemen upstairs.

The fire was now behind them, cutting them off in a wall of backdraft. Hartsook's job that night was to keep checking the hose – for firefighters, the lifeline – and Hartsook waited on the ground, in case backup was needed.

The man who had disappeared leading the teams inside the house was Hartsook's mentor, Assistant Chief Sam Anders. When Hartsook's parents divorced, Anders had taken the teen under his wing, driven him to the junior firefighter meetings, taken charge of his training, was best man at his wedding.

So as Hartsook stood below and felt the wind picking up, stoking the blaze like a bellows, he pulled the water hose as a signal to Anders. The hose was slack and he realized: The fire was so hot inside the house that it had melted the double-jacketed polymer hose in two. Hartsook was holding a severed lifeline in his hands.

Sam!

Instinctively, Hartsook craned his neck to the second floor, nothing but black soot. Out a side window tumbled seven of the eight trapped firemen. All but Sam Anders. Hartsook and a rescue team raced into the collapsing house. There was no trace of Anders.

Meanwhile, there was commotion outside. Through

the oily black smoke from burning shingles, Colfax engine company had spotted a flashlight shining through the soot.

It was attached to a fireman – Anders, who had fled through an upstairs front window, fallen spread-eagle on his back and was now dangling on the steep tin roof, looking back at the burning house.

Colfax company raised a ladder and picked Anders off the roof before it caved in. Chief Newman made a command decision. Let this one burn.

❄ ❄ ❄

It is hard to say, exactly, what goes through a firefighter's brain when that distinctive high radio frequency, followed by a low tone, comes over the scanner, then opens the channel.

"Station 15, for a 10-50 at Linville Road and Highway 150..."

Whatever the transformation those tones from the scanner brought about, Clay Hartsook wanted in. One minute his grandfathers, his uncles and their friends would be shooting pool or grilling hot dogs, then everything would change with a call.

"Seeing the trucks leave, lights and sirens going, seeing people go from a calm everyday thing to 110 percent," he says, "that was for me."

Even older firemen such as Roger Howerton, who joined Oak Ridge in 1958 and answered calls for 40 years, still confess to a tingle of adrenaline when they hear the station's call over the scanner, or see a company engine go by.

But what captivates a child in a toy helmet or excites

a teenager craving adventure is not what makes a man join the 82nd Airborne, following three classmates killed in battle.

At age 21, Hartsook, an only child, announced to his mother that he was joining the Army, wanting to "kick it up a notch." His mother, having been a Special Forces wife, knew the questions to ask.

What did he sign up for?

"Infantry."

Direct or indirect?

"Direct."

Clay, why?

"Somebody's gotta do it."

So off he went to Fort Benning, Ga., where he was a Distinguished Honor Graduate in boot camp, put in for airborne, and is, at this writing, en route to Iraq, to be security detail for the Third Brigade Command.

And like climbing the stairs of a 96-year-old house engulfed in flames, it sounds like a dangerous job.

But that's where the training comes in. Pfc. Clay Hartsook knows the emergency dispatch by heart, from the alpha to the omega.

And once the call for backup comes in, there is not a hose man in the world who has ever been able to roll over and go back to sleep.

— December 7, 2008

A Hawk Soars:
Victory Over the Wounds of War

❄

At night when the hospital wing is quiet, when he's rewound his last Kung-Fu video and dealt the last hand of an impenetrable Vietnamese card game, sometimes he tells me a story.

It unfolds long ago, but not that long. Far away, but not that far. It starts in a mountain village, with a spray of AK-47s and the whistle of a mortar he can still feel across the back of his neck. Mother dead, father dead, two sisters and a brother, everybody dead.

A child left alone toddles off into the perilous shelter of the jungle, at the mercy of wild animals, bone-chilling monsoons and blinding-hot droughts.

He makes his way along a strange, barren mountain-top. He sees a family of elephants cross a waterfall. He befriends a screeching monkey, just to remember how to talk. He kills a fat snake and cooks the meat over the fire. And always, year after year, soldiers are on the hunt.

That's why, in the fluorescent cool of his Greensboro hospital room, he laughs at the stuntman antics of Jackie Chan and Jean-Claude Van Damme, laughs until it hurts. Because unlike Chan and Van Damme, Y Bler Buonya's story is true.

The sixth floor of Moses Cone, the cancer ward, is no place for a young man, and Bler (pronounced BLAIR) is by far the youngest man here.

He's only about 20, his doctors think, but the plastic band around his slender brown wrist gives his date of birth as 1969 – a date somebody picked out of a hat when he arrived in Greensboro as a political refugee five years back.

I met Bler not long after that, and I first heard the story.

"One day I stayed by myself, and suddenly there was nobody to stay close to me," the story began. "It came very quickly, but THEY didn't see me...."

The year was sometime in the late 1970s, well after the U.S. withdrew from Vietnam. Communist government troops were purging the countryside of anyone suspected of having been on the wrong side.

The annihilation of young Bler's village in the province of Kontum was part of a campaign of terror against the Montagnards. These were ethnic highland tribes whose bid for independence continued long after the Vietnam War ended, long after most Americans had relegated Vietnam to the history books.

The orphaned Bler, scooped up by Montagnard rebel soldiers, spent about 15 years of his life on the run in the rugged jungles of central Vietnam and Cambodia. He survived on roots and berries, drank from mountain streams, and learned to shoot an AK-47 and use the hit-and-run tactics of the guerilla soldiers.

When he stepped off a plane in Greensboro in 1992, the Montagnards' David-and-Goliath struggle against Vietnam had become a thorn in the side for U.N. negotiators trying to secure peace between Vietnam and Cambodia.

And so the only thing to do was convince the rebel Montagnards to lay down their arms and resettle in the

United States, all 200 of them. After 15 years in the wild, sleeping with one eye open, living without coins or calendars or doctors, the boy for the first time slept in a bed, wore shoes and went to school to learn to read and write.

No one can say what caused the cancer – Burkitt's Lymphoma, in Bler's case – but he was not the first in the group. Across the courtyard at the run-down apartments where some of the Montagnards live, a young mother died of cancer, and two of the men died of cancer.

Was it a predisposition? Was it Agent Orange, the defoliant used by one side in the war, or Yellow Rain, the lethal nerve agent used by the other?

Whatever the cause, by the time he was treated this spring and summer, the cancer twisted like a vine through his abdomen. His lean, strong limbs shrank. His glistening black hair fell away from the chemotherapy. The disease made the marrow in his bones expand, and at night his teeth ached.

Between the spinal taps, the sucking chest pump, the IV drip and the morphine, he dreamed he was fighting with elephants. Furious and stampeding.

One July morning on the ledge of his sixth-floor window, a large brown hawk landed and glared in at him, fierce and protective. It sat motionless for hours – all the nurses came to see it – something that didn't belong here, any more than this brown-eyed boy out of the jungle.

And then one morning last week, at another in an endless blur of medical appointments, Dr. Brad Sherrill opened a file and looked Bler in the eye. The cancer was in remission. The elephant fell dead at last, and out in the green wild, the hawk soared again.

– September 14, 1997

Code Name:
"Operation Powder Blue"

❄

They make an odd pair at Special Forces reunions – a taut, 60-ish Asian everyone calls "Pedro" and an older white man with a mustache and a catch in his gait, whether from the stroke he had last year or that last jump at Fort Bragg, when his chute didn't open all the way.

No, you wouldn't automatically put the two together or guess that they shared a role in an untold tale of the Vietnam War. It was a story written before they knew it was a story, and for 25 years, it remained untold.

It had to. It was classified.

❄ ❄ ❄

The code name was "Operation Powder Blue," a strike force that was to be the first U.S.-led helicopter assault of the Vietnam War. Except it wasn't a war yet. Not on paper.

So-called American "advisers" such as Special Forces Master Sgt. Art Fields, under CIA orders to train counter insurgency against the Communists, didn't wear uniforms and kept their side arms concealed.

All that changed after Oct. 15, 1962, the assault that would bring things into the open, lose the advisers their clandestine status, put them back in uniform and under military assistance command for "Operation Switchback." But here, we're getting ahead of the story.

Fields, a Korean War vet who was born in the Army hospital at Bragg and liked to tell people that he wore khaki diapers as a baby, had arrived in Southeast Asia in August 1962 for a tour of Vietnam's Central Highlands.

The highlands were rugged and remote "Indian country," where the Communists from North Vietnam and anti-Communists from South Vietnam clashed. Caught in the middle were the Montagnards, a moniker the aboriginal tribesmen gained from the previous Western power to fight the Communists, the French.

This was "Indian country" in more ways than one: Like the Native Americans, the Polynesian-descended racial minority of Montagnards were being displaced and exterminated. After a thousand years in isolation, using elephants for transport and water buffalo for farming, the Montagnards now saw their thatched longhouses on stilts being burned, villages bombed and lands taken.

Into this picture stepped the Americans. Determined to stop Vietnam from being the latest Communist domino in the region, they made a promise.

"They said, 'Support us, and we won't leave you,'" recalls Greensboro resident Y-Tin Hwing, 63, who at 17 became one of the first Montagnard recruits, and not by chance. Schooled by missionaries, he spoke English. "The Americans said, 'We'll back you up, protect your family, your land, your rights.'"

All through the countryside, from the 17th parallel to the Mekong Delta, Special Forces teams were training Montagnards by the thousands, with Fields' team alone training 86 villages. Like their Viet Cong counterparts, the Montagnard fighters initially wore black pajamas instead of camouflage. They were armed, but with older non-U.S.-issued weapons such as Mausers and Schmeissers from World War II.

The advisers, dispatched out of Okinawa and flown in unmarked C-47 transports piloted by Taiwanese nationals, had hacked their way up the elephant paths to the highland villages. There, they were greeted by loin-clothed chiefs, the beating of drums and gongs, and always, the ceremonial feast with jars of rice wine sipped through bamboo straws.

It was during this time that Fields met "a 17-year-old, fuzzy-faced kid" they nicknamed Pedro – to the GIs, he looked more Mexican than he did Vietnamese – and they paid him the princely sum of 4,500 dong (about $3) to be an interpreter, helping the team train the tribesmen, leading inspections to the Cambodian border, and ultimately, carrying out Powder Blue.

The mission was to destroy a Viet Cong training camp, but once this was complete, a reconnaissance plane flying low over the site in broad daylight would be shot down, causing the first casualty of the war of a Special Forces officer, as well as two Air Force crewmen.

Watching the plane go down in flames, Fields, his young interpreter and their team raced to the crash site, then spent a long, dark night waiting for an evacuation helicopter to be sent from Pleiku the next morning. As Viet Cong harassed the circle of 400 U.S.-led Montagnards guarding the crash site, Fields had Pedro give the order:

"Anything that moves inside or outside this perimeter," Y-Tin told the Montagnards, "will be shot."

The next day, they tracked a band of Viet Cong to a

straw shack on the edge of a rice paddy, surrounded them and killed them. Inside the shack, Fields found the weapon that had been used to shoot the plane.

Like a hand beckoning from the grave, it had a ghostly history to it. It was a BAR, a Browning Automatic Rifle, of World War II vintage. Likely left behind in the subsequent French war in Indochina, it was in poor condition but still fired.

Now, the quiet deployment of "advisers" was public knowledge, and the cycle of history in Vietnam was about to turn again. Within a year, there were 21,000 of them in the country. Within two years, the massive escalation of America's longest war had begun.

❄ ❄ ❄

It was 1987 when Y-Tin Hwing walked unsteadily out the gates of the "re-education camp" in what used to be North Vietnam. His friend Art Fields was long gone, leaving Vietnam in 1968. South Vietnam fell in 1975, and Y-Tin had been imprisoned in a camp where a dozen inmates, locked up as enemies of the regime, died of starvation in a typical day.

They were forgotten. Washington, which to this day has never officially recognized their service, made no effort to get them out. And once back in their own villages – those lucky enough to survive "re-education" – they were like ghosts.

"My son didn't even call me 'father.' Didn't even know me. He was 10 when I left. When I got back, he was 22," Y-Tin said. "My wife met somebody else."

Still, there was one bond unbroken. Y-Tin managed in 1994 to get a letter smuggled out, to the man who had been Fields' first lieutenant in Powder Blue. The lieutenant was now retired and a stockbroker in Key Biscayne, Fla. He offered to help Y-Tin with an exit visa, and the Montagnard eventually joined fellow exiles in Greensboro.

And so it was that by 2002, the man they called Pedro found himself at a Special Forces memorial at Fort Bragg, looking into the eyes of an old white man with a mustache.

"I'm looking for Pedro," the American said. "Are you Pedro?"

"Are you Arthur Fields?" the Montagnard replied.

What were the odds? Forty years since they'd been separated – a Green Beret born at the Army hospital, a Montagnard half a world from home – the two men stood back and looked at each other.

They started to laugh.

– December 3, 2006

The Phoenix of Pearl Harbor

❄

Making a long story short isn't so much the problem.

No, when it comes to the story of Johnny Stanley, the trick is knowing where it begins and where it ends.

I guess it begins on the morning of his 22nd birthday – Dec. 7, 1941 – when he's in the shower on the USS Phoenix and scrambles topside to see Pearl Harbor in flames around him.

On the other hand, we could scroll ahead about 60 years, a lifetime after his first wife vanishes with the three girls, after he gives up trying to track them down, remarries, and is finally a widower living on a pension. When one day a knock comes on the door of his trailer at the edge of town, and standing there is this pretty blond woman he's never seen before. And yet – there is something so familiar about her.

Are you Mr. Stanley? Johnny Stanley? she says. Do you know who I am?

He takes a step back, and that's when he realizes. It's the eyes, the eyes of the little blond child in the black-and-white portrait on his dresser, eyes that have looked back at him, trusting, questioning, every morning and night all these years.

Yes, I think I do, he tells the stranger. I think you're my Debbie.

❄ ❄ ❄

He wakes up on a gray December morning, pours himself a bowl of cereal and watches the squirrels outside, burying hazelnuts. He's an old man now, and he never really expected to live through this many more birthdays – retiring from selling Singer sewing machines, burying his second wife 10 years ago, living alone here in a quiet trailer park south of Greensboro.

So maybe it's the solitude, or having no set schedule to occupy his mind, but some mornings in that moment before he wakes up, it comes to him like a vision – the smoke, the noise, the confusion – as if it's all happening again, and he's back on the Phoenix. It's the Sunday morning he turned 22, the first day of the war.

His brother is in Honolulu with the Army at the time, so they're taking Johnny out for his birthday to the most expensive place they can find, the Royal Hawaiian Hotel.

He's been a signal operator for more than a year aboard the light cruiser, sending his parents in Leaksville a picture postcard of the Phoenix, calling it "a swell ship."

As he showers early the morning of Dec. 7, he hears the sirens of an air raid drill, only they're too fast. Then he hears the bugle call. Air defense. Battle stations.

On deck is chaos – fighter planes diving and strafing, explosions from torpedoes, sailors on nearby ships diving into the water, surfacing in pools of burning oil, then disappearing again in the black waves.

Side by side, the Tennessee and the West Virginia are on fire, belching smoke. From a turret, a gunner on the Phoenix fires one of the 6-inch guns at a plane with a Japanese Rising Sun on the wing. They watched it crash in the sugar cane fields on Oahu.

Then come the explosions from the Arizona, where crowds of sailors have arrived for Sunday Mass just as the attack starts. As planes try to shoot the men on the top deck, everything on the Arizona burns – the sides, the bulkheads. A series of blasts catapults blocks of white-hot steel clear to Ford Island.

With the attack targeting the bigger ships and battle groups, the 10,000-ton Phoenix, moored by itself out in the harbor, escapes damage and is among the first to come about and leave Pearl Harbor on its own power.

As they sail out of the ruined harbor to go on patrol, the crew of the Phoenix passes by motor launches full of dead sailors who were supposed to go ashore on leave. Soon, wooden caskets are piled 10 high, up and down the beach.

For the next four years, always sailing toward the sunrise or sunset, the Phoenix takes them to Guadalcanal, Los Negros, Mindanao, Leyte Gulf, Corregidor, Ceber City, and eventually back to Pearl Harbor, where it comes to rest on the last day of the war at the same two buoys where it had been moored on the first.

Ultimately, they head back through the Panama Canal and on to Philadelphia, but that isn't the end for the Phoenix. The Argentine navy later buys the cruiser, and in a place called the Falkland Islands, under the orders of a prime minister named Mrs. Thatcher, the Phoenix sinks and at last joins the Arizona, waiting an ocean away at the bottom of the sea.

In a tattered manila envelope, along with his discharge documents, Johnny Stanley keeps the newspaper clipping about the sinking of the Phoenix, with the headline "500 Men Feared Lost."

And there you have it. After escaping Pearl Harbor unscathed and helping drive back the Japanese fleet at the Surigao Strait, the Phoenix perishes in a battle over some rocky, godforsaken territory nobody has ever heard of.

Destiny will wait – but only for so long. At times, what appears to be the end of the story is only an intermission.

❄ ❄ ❄

As she climbs the wooden steps to the stranger's trailer, nervous, aware of her husband watching her from the car, Deborah Cabral has remembered to bring two things along – a birth certificate, showing that a man named John Stanley is her father, and the little scrapbook about her father that she's held onto for 50 years.

Her maternal grandmother had made the book for Debbie, and that never seemed to add up. Why would a man's mother-in-law speak so fondly of him, while his ex-wife had always told their three daughters that Johnny Stanley was a no-good, never cared about his children, never asked about them or tried to provide?

Debbie was 2 when her parents divorced in 1952, and other than the scrapbook and birth certificate, she has a single memory of her father. He's pushing her on a swing at some relative's farm. A chicken scurries under the swing and squawks when the child's shoe bumps it. Frightened, Debbie starts to cry, and her father scoops her up in his arms. And everybody laughs.

So all her life, it's an unanswered question. Could he be that bad? Where do I get my sense of humor? My nature? Not from her mother, she says.

For a long time, she leaves it alone, lets it lie. And then one night, she's at this law enforcement banquet for her husband's firm, and she's making conversation with one of the guests. Debbie brings up her father, for some reason.

He probably never even thinks about us, she remarks.

And the dinner guest, a retired cop she's never seen before and will never again, gets a funny look on his face.

Oh, yes, he thinks about you, the man assures her. The closer he gets to death, the more he thinks about you.

Which brings her from her home in Alexandria, Va., to the doorstep of the trailer south of Greensboro a couple of autumns back,

Looking back on it, maybe Johnny Stanley always knew this day would come. He'd kept all his records – yellowed receipts from the 1950s, showing the child support payments he made through the Clerk of Court. And invoices from those detective agencies that advertise on TV – "Find anyone, guaranteed" – for $89 per try, not quite the caliber of private investigators Debbie's husband would ultimately enlist.

So of course, Johnny never could find them – his ex-wife had moved west, remarried, changed her name. As years became decades, he slowly let go. The pain, the lack, was just part of his life.

What, then, do you say, when you're holding her again, here at the end, or what seemed like the end?

It's all like a waking dream. His only three children in his life again, grandchildren he didn't know he had, even great-grandchildren, filling up his empty address book, filling up photo albums as fast as he can buy them.

Of course, no telling how much time they have. The daughter in California writes him long, long letters, and Debbie visits a lot. She had him up for Thanksgiving, and tried to buy him plane tickets, but he always rides the train.

The fact is, he hasn't wanted to fly since he saw the wings with the red Rising Sun the morning of his 22nd birthday, Dec. 7, 1941.

If fate can be this kind to one man, why tempt it now?

— December 7, 2003

PART 4

Game Faces

What was in the Professor's Box?

❄

I don't know, maybe some stories start out as mysteries only to end up that way, too. Maybe Gordon Walton is one of them.

He was tall and spindly, British, mannerly, precise. People used to call him "The Professor" as kind of a friendly joke – winos by the railroad tracks, cops who walked the downtown Greensboro beat, librarians who fetched him academic journals, receptionists who dutifully kept him from coming upstairs at the newspaper.

But the fact is, his nickname was no joke. Walton was an Oxford-trained physicist and a former university professor who lived on the streets of Greensboro for much of the past 30 years. He was a running apparition. A reminder of something you couldn't put your finger on. A riddle you might put aside for awhile, but could never quite escape.

Hard to miss in his orange knit cap – bleak winter or blazing summer – he carried a large cardboard box out in front of him, as if looking for a place to put it down. Anybody who saw him had at least one question: What was in the box?

Well, after Walton died a couple of weeks back on his 76th birthday – in the hospital and not on the street – we finally found out what was in the box. Sort of.

Last Monday there was a memorial service for Walton at the soup kitchen – the only one they've ever had at

Urban Ministry. A few dozen people signed the guest book, and most of them had never met before. Walton, they soon learned, was the only thread they had in common.

There was a physics professor from A&T, where Walton taught after leaving Greensboro College, and earlier UCLA. Beside the physicist sat a branch librarian who used to wait on Walton. And a man from a gift wrap company which periodically supplied Walton with a new box. Two guys came from Greensboro Self Storage, where Walton kept his belongings and methodically paid his rent the first of each month – in person when he was up and around, by mail after he was on crutches.

A woman showed up who dated Walton before he had his breakdown, which somebody described as an obsessive-compulsive disorder. And there was a Catholic monsignor, real old-school, who lately was helping Walton study to join the church. The priest got a catch in his throat trying to comfort the odd assortment of mourners.

But most odd was seeing the contents of Walton's box carefully laid out on a long table by his friend Betty Rogers, arranged into a story as best they could be.

Among the photos he carried were color postcards of Bexhill-on-Sea, Walton's hometown southeast of London. Black and white portraits of his mother and his father, a schoolmaster. Walton at Oxford, beaming in his tux, surrounded by friends, celebrating some milestone – maybe his PhD.

Then the picture changes. The papers include his parents' death certificates. His adoption papers, which cousins back in England say he only discovered as a teen. A passport, a postcard of an ocean liner, a series of wallet-size portraits in which his expression turns guarded and suspicious.

In the 1950s he wrote pioneering articles on the atmospheric ozone, the scattering of cosmic rays and absorption of ultra-violet sunlight. But by the time he left Greensboro College and later A&T in 1970, he could barely speak to his physics students. He'd stand with his back to them, writing out problems, muttering to the blackboard.

And for all those years on the street, spurning treatment, spurning help, he was a puzzle to strangers but a bigger puzzle to those who knew the story behind the face. It was a puzzle all in pieces – genius, madness, the fine line between.

"People say, 'I'll see you,' and then I have to prepare and get ready," Walton once told a colleague. "And then they don't show up."

Only in the past year did people who knew him see his face change again. Still confused and blurry, Walton nevertheless was calmer, talkative, accepting of help. Before he died, he made up a Christmas card list, and agonized over a personal greeting, striking through each attempt:

~~I am going to wish you...~~

~~I am about to wish you...~~

Finally he wrote one he kept:
Merry Christmas, and best wishes in 2000. Gordon.

– December 12, 1999

A Blue Plate to Say Grace Over

❋

The last anybody heard, Jan was a blackjack dealer in Vegas and her father, the one who named the diner after her, had sold out and moved to Myrtle Beach.

But the house Jan's father built – Jan's House, the oldest diner in Greensboro – is still buzzing along on West Market, the neon sign lit 24 hours a day, seven days a week. Master Burgers at 6 a.m., Belly Buster breakfasts at midnight – anything you want, anytime you want it – including New Year's, Christmas and, you guessed it, Thanksgiving Day.

Bordered by a Sonic Drive In, where you can eat in your car, and Biscuitville, where you can eat while you drive away, it's a throwback with an unlikely benefactor.

Owner Margie Walker is 36, has a master's degree in education, and walked into an all-night classroom when she bought Jan's House from Troy Blythe in 1999. The reason is, you never quite know who will sit down at the counter: It might be Congressman Howard Coble, when he's in town, or some guy in a tattered seed cap.

"Then that guy will leave," says Walker, "and you find out he's worth six million dollars. Just because he worked hard."

Not that hard work always gets you there. In a shopping center where Southern Cash Advance replaced a print shop and Aaron Rents moved into the old Kroger,

Jan's House looks out on a suddenly chilly scene. What economists might call a "spiral effect."

Directly across Market Street, the Flav-O-Rich dairy is shut down. So is the Guilford Mills plant up the street. And the Timco mechanics have been scarce.

That's when you thank your stars for loyalty. A businessman who comes in every day for a cup of coffee at 3 p.m. A nursing student who spreads out in a booth with her anatomy book. And the big guy with the pony tail who works next door at Dizzy G's and gets his three squares at Jan's House.

He ambles back to his table to leave a tip, but not fast enough for Lola Cox, a waitress with a raspy voice and a bouffant.

"Where's my DOLLAR?" demands Cox, eliciting a muttered reply that amuses the heating repairmen at the next booth but leaves Cox undeterred.

"Don't even go there. I want my DOLLAR."

Each shift is a different slice of the pie. Days are working people, like the sportswriter who is so unwavering in his order – two up, bacon and grits – that they start cracking the eggs when they see him drive up.

Dinner is older couples and widows. The night shift is for the two groups out on the town: young people who have been to the bars and the clubs, and cops and security guards on their break.

"People who work alone, with no one to talk to, they like to come in here for some conversation," says Walker,

Jan's House
2007

who first ate at Jan's House as a college student.

What she saw – what she sees – is "a microcosm of what Greensboro should be." A city that can still seem like a town if you look at it in the right light – a neon light that says "24 HOURS."

"Without that human interaction, it could be Charlotte, it could be Orlando," Walker says. "You eat here a few times, before you know it, you'll know the person on your left and the person on your right. It's not about the food. It's about the people."

– November 21, 2001

Big George and the 38-Foot Tree

❄

Maybe the closest thing up to now is this one Christmas morning back in L.A. – George is 8 years and his old man tells him to go out and get the paper.

George walks out on the porch, and he can't believe his eyes. There's a bike sitting there – a brand spanking new Schwinn Sting Ray – gold with a white banana seat, monkey bars, springs on the front end, even a horn.

He goes racing up and down the street, honking the horn, popping wheelies, and until recently, it's about the most triumphant day of his life.

See, George Tricas is 40 now, and there's a lot of years in between with not a lot of triumph. His parents divorce, his mom is an addict and she dies when George is 11. He moves into a boys home at age 13, and to prove something to his old man, he ends up staying there until he's 18.

Then come 20 lost years in and of prison – drinking, drugs, living in his car, bumming from house to house for a shower and a place to wash his clothes. Three and four days at a time with no sleep, until he passes out somewhere.

This goes on until his own friends don't want him around. Until all his petty crimes add up to the possibility of 25 years to life. Until he reaches for a lifeline.

And that's how he winds up here – three years later,

clean as a whistle – fixing me a cup of coffee at the Delancey Street Christmas tree stand behind St. Pius schoolyard in Greensboro.

The people in the program for recovering addicts call him "Big George," but he's just a stocky, average-size guy with a quiet face and clear hazel eyes. He runs the Delancey Street moving business, which is how the residential program gets much of its income, and every year it's George's job to drive the truck to the mountains and bring back Christmas trees to sell.

To supply this stand on Cornwallis and the other lot at Guilford College Road near Market Street, it will take George three trips in the tractor-trailer, leaving at 4 a.m. for Bald Mountain.

He gets there at sunrise to start loading, and it's cold enough on the farm near Boone that you can see a deer's breath. George brings back 400 fresh-cut No. 1 Fraser firs at a time, and he and couple of other guys unroll them and put them on stands under the lights.

The rest of the year, George is in school on a Rotary Club scholarship, studying heating and air conditioning, puzzling over wiring schematics and solid state boards, sitting next to people half his age.

He almost gave up on it until he talked to his brother – he's been back in touch with his family since he got off drugs – and his brother explained something about electricity. It always takes the easiest path to where it's going – like water, he said. Or like people, I guess.

And George keeps thinking about the time he's wasted, and how he could have done all this years ago – learned a trade, gotten engaged to this woman he's met, started drawing plans to build his own house.

But then he tells me about this tree he picked up the

Monday before Thanksgiving – a tree so big it took a special trip, riding home with a load 14 feet wide.

It's the tree that goes in front of the Wrangler headquarters on North Elm Street every Christmas, and this year they found it in Todd Valley, growing in front of this couple's house.

The husband and wife say they planted it almost three decades ago – right around the time George was moving into the Good Samaritan foster home – and now it stands 38 feet tall.

The amazing thing is how quietly a tree that size comes down – they put a big boom on top, tether lines to either side, and ease it down in the grass with hardly a sound.

And like it or not, regret it or not, these are the things you notice when you're on your second chance. The stillness of the morning in Todd Valley. How hot the coffee feels in your hand through a thin plastic cup. The slant of the sunset, so bright it just about blinds you on these last few Sundays in deep December.

Out here until 10 o'clock every night, George will sell every tree he can, then give the last few away on Christmas Eve.

And somewhere between the prick of pine needles and the sharp scent of cuttings for the wreaths, he's going to see a boy shopping for a tree with his parents, and he'll get that feeling again. Like his first ride on a gold Schwinn Sting Ray with a white banana seat.

– December 5, 1999

Lo-Ray's House in Town

❄

So they finally did it. They sold the horse farm out on McConnell Road, bought a townhouse near the Taj Ma-Teeter, and hired an auctioneer to nail up a sign at the entrance to Lo-Ray Farm and place an ad with the legal notices.

"SOLD FARM, MOVED TO TOWNHOUSE," it says, then lists everything they own from the Bush Hog mower, manure spreader, bird dog training table and bull emasculator down to the Christmas decorations and the old copper bathtub with the solid oak trim.

And like the husband and wife in the TV show "Green Acres," where they leave their Park Avenue penthouse and move to Hooterville, I suppose you could say Raymond and Lorena Copeland have mixed emotions. There are his, on the one hand. And on the other hand, there are hers.

Raymond was out in the tack room Tuesday morning, hanging rows of oiled saddles, bridles and halters, as a clatter of acorns fell on the roof of the old barn. He paused to drink in the October morning, the first frost still in the air.

"I love cold weather. That's when I horseback ride a lot, and run my bird dogs," the retired veterinarian said, wiping his brow with the sleeve of his muddy coveralls. "When this auction is over, I'm just gonna put my head under a pillow and cry. It's like losing my right arm. But don't tell her that."

"Her" meaning Lorena, who was at that moment inside the old farmhouse, sorting glasses, pictures and trinkets for the Saturday auction.

When they moved here 46 years ago and started raising the twins, it was just a rundown old place with a pot-bellied stove and some chicken coops. During the years they kept cutting doors and adding on. But even with a furnace on each floor, even with her jacket on, Lorena Copeland shivered.

"It's fine in the summer, but I'm such a cold-natured person," she said, looking out at the swimming pool that was covered over, and the patio littered with oak leaves.

"Now, I'm a having a ball – I love my new place in town. I can get in the car and zip here, zip there. There's everything we need. A dry cleaners. A new Chick-Fil-A. He's going to have a hard adjustment to make," she said, glancing out toward the barn, "but I won't. Just don't tell him that."

But before we inventory the rest of what Raymond is about to part with – the five setters and Brittany spaniels, the pregnant Thercheron mare, the pony wagon they once used for picnics, the Snapper mower, the brand new Sundowner horse trailer – let's back up a few years.

It's June of '53, he and Lorena are just married, and Raymond is just finishing veterinary school and studying for his board exams. On their honeymoon, he lugs so many books along that the desk clerk at the motor inn gives him a spare room for studying.

And once they buy the old Cobb place on McConnell Road – where you can still read "Perry F. Cobb, 1905," carved into the side of a feed barn – Raymond spends his spare time mowing the pastures and getting the hay in barn, tending his vegetable gardens, mending fences, training bird dogs.

In between, the couple travels to horse shows and horse sales – "and mules," Lorena recalls, wincing. Raymond accumulates enough horses that he wires a closed-circuit camera from the barn to their TV in the house, to monitor the mares when they go into labor.

He's been selling them one by one, but is keeping Pusher Boy, a speckled walking horse who gallops from the far side of the pasture when Raymond whistles. And he might keep a dog or two. But as for the butter churn and the post hole digger, the dog cages, coal buckets and cattle tagging supplies – you can only fit so much in a townhouse.

It's funny, every time he talks about selling the farm, people ask him the same thing: "Are you crazy?"

Of course, he's not. Stay married to someone for 48 years – someone who goes to mule sales with you and doesn't complain when you wire the TV in the bedroom to the mare's stall in the barn – and, well... It's just one of those sacrifices you make.

– October 10, 2001

Golden Age:
Life as a Script in Development

✳

He was the TV writer who named the pig "Arnold." The one who grew weary of "Gilligan's Island" guest stars getting shipwrecked every week, so he wrote an episode where a surfer rides in on a tsunami.

If you ask him to, Greensboro resident Lou Huston, 86, can unreel tales all day from his career in the heyday of shows like "Petticoat Junction," "Green Acres" and "The Beverly Hillbillies."

But if you want a yarn with everything – plot twists, character development, epic sweep and sheer staying power – none comes close to Huston's own story. It's how he got from Point A, a clever, successful writer on the brink of self-destruction, to Point B, the oldest member of the substance abuse therapy staff at Fellowship Hall, where he's worked for 22 years.

This is one of those rare two-picture deals where the sequel turns out better than the original. And like any decent storyline, it's got a cliffhanger.

It begins late one September night in 1957, when Lou has been to a party on the beach in Malibu. He's getting a ride back to his home in the San Fernando Valley – he totaled his own car in a drunken crash a month earlier – and they're coming around a mountain curve.

Somebody makes a joke, and the last thing Lou hears is the

driver saying, That reminds me... And the last thing he sees is a broken white picket fence as they go careening toward a 100-foot precipice, stopped only by a tree on the way down.

The car hits hard enough to throw the passengers clear and knock them unconscious. At a firehouse nearby, somebody hears the crash and gets there in time to keep Lou from bleeding to death.

So he's snatched from the jaws once again – as in the pulp he might have churned out in his radio days for "The Whistler," "Suspense" or "Space Patrol."

Except after all this – the blown deadlines, the bounced checks at liquor stores, the blackouts and the crushing hangovers when he can't remember how he got home – he doesn't grasp the theme. Out of the hospital after the mountain crash, Lou tells a doctor: You're not talking to an alcoholic. I haven't had a drink in 36 hours.

Of course, consider the times. There's no Betty Ford Clinic. No stars giving interviews about their battles with addiction. Not that people don't do flagrant, reckless things. They just never make it into print.

For instance, the opera star Lou goes to hear at an oceanside concert. Outside the hall, the star sits in a convertible with a bottle, multiple sheets to the wind. When a man in the crowd faints, the star picks him up and dangles him by the ankles off the pier to revive him.

Or the time at the ritzy Ciro's, when a well-known director and female star, both drunk, play out their version of Sodom and Gomorrah in full view of the dance floor. Frantic, the waiters pull starched tablecloths off empty tables and hold up a makeshift curtain.

But even if the word "alcoholic" had been part of the vernacular – and not just for Bowery bums – does an alcoholic ever recognize the signs? Sure, Lou had seen the gritty, groundbreaking movie "The Lost Weekend." Ray Milland plays a bingeing, hallucinating alcoholic, and the famous line is a hospital orderly telling him, You'll be back. They all come back.

And Lou is sitting in the theater, thinking, This is a wonderful movie, but I'll be glad when it's over so I can go get a drink.

Not that he doesn't have flashes of guilt. He won't go to guild meetings for fear of getting drunk in front of his peers. Likewise, he stops seeing close friends. And the time he rams his car into a streetlight and wakes up with a head injury, he asks a nurse, Are there any charges?

She says, no, not yet – thinking he's asking about his bill. But even in 1950s Hollywood, reality sometimes intrudes. For example, when you go careening off a 100-foot mountain pass. And survive.

This time, Lou hears a voice – bigger than his own, bigger than Cecil B. DeMille's. The voice says, If you have another drink, disaster will strike. He gets into a self-help program, goes on with his career.

But TV changes in the '70s, and jobs dry up for the old sitcom writers, so Lou does what they used to call a "switch." The gag writer ends up doing a documentary on alcoholism, another on teen drinking, then a counseling job, then a column for recovering addicts called "Lou's Cues."

He still gets around at 86, but these days he feels like Tim Conway's shuffling Grampa on "Carol Burnett." He'd take five minutes to cross the room, then turn back to get his glasses, breaking up his straight man, Harvey Korman, every time.

Like Conway, the guy who named Arnold the Pig is still getting laughs in the reruns.

– October 29, 2000

Death of a Boy:
Someday isn't Soon Enough

❄

T alk is cheap, and getting cheaper by the minute
while we stand here on the future site of "Hope
VI," beside the trash-strewn ditch that was 13-year-
old Tiawan Norfleet's front yard.

The elder who preached the funeral last weekend,
big bear of a man with gray whiskers and a Yellow cab
he drives for his day job, abruptly knocks the car with
his knuckles and then composes himself.

"I hate that it took this to get us together," the elder,
James Byrd says, facing out toward the infamous Lincoln
Grove and Morningside Homes, soon to be redeveloped
into the massive $75 million Hope VI.

With Byrd is Pat Gill-Galbert, who started the com-
paratively miniscule program for boys where Tiawan
was doing so well – singing baritone in the Guilford
Boys Choir, dreaming of playing pro football.

In fact, he showed so much progress in Making It
Upstream that counselors used him as a model – that is,
until the program's state application process dragged on
so long that the money ran out.

Gill-Galbert takes off her sunglasses, rubs her eyes
wearily and still musters outrage.

"He just fell through the cracks," she says flatly, looking back at the dingy block of apartments where Tiawan

lived on Dunbar Street, apartments about to be condemned for Hope VI. "If you try to help these kids, your programs don't count."

But I'm not here to ask about social policy or budget allocations or bureaucracy. I just want to know the cause of death of a 13-year-old boy, one that didn't make the news, didn't warrant an investigation, didn't attract much notice at all.

You see, Tiawan Norfleet didn't die from a gunshot. And pending an autopsy result, the coroner didn't suspect it was drug-related, either – although anytime someone this young from a neighborhood this poor dies, the rumors fly.

But he could have died from any number of causes. He had severe asthma. He was battling a weight problem, and had recent surgery on his legs, bowed from when he was hit by a car at age 9, continually in pain from never having healed correctly.

He was staying with his aunt two Sundays back at St. James Homes, just up Eugene Street from the flagrant drive-through drug market known as "The Block." That night at 8:45 he complained that he couldn't breathe, he got sick to his stomach, and two hours later, he was dead.

So as for a cause, take your pick.

"A lot of his problem was environmental – poverty, mainly," said Dwight Jones, the former Making It Upstream program coordinator who knew Tiawan as "Big T."

"He lived in an apartment with holes in the floor, and raw sewage out in the ditch. Or he stays at his aunt's house, where he sees kids outside selling drugs all day. And that's all he sees."

When Tiawan came into the program a year ago, he barely spoke to the counselors or the other boys. He was

self-conscious about being sickly and overweight, and
got in trouble for fighting at school and cursing at a
teacher.

But gradually, Jones and the other counselors
watched the boy change. He grew more confident, and
started doing push-ups to get in shape. Last summer, he
sang the lead for the Boys' Choir – "I Believe I Can Fly"
– for hundreds of people at the reopening of Four
Seasons Town Centre.

Jones encouraged the boy's dreams of football – "Big
T. Norfleet from Greensboro," he recalls in a mock
sportscaster's voice – but the program got to be a "some-
timey" thing.

Sometimes there was transportation. Sometimes there
was money to pay the staff. And some day, if they held
on long enough, the licenses and permits and applica-
tions would all be in order for Making It Upstream to
open a home for boys like Tiawan in Greensboro.

But just like Hope VI, which one day promises to
remake Dunbar Street and the rest of his old neighborhood, Tiawan won't be around to see it.

For now, we're standing beside a ditch full of trash
and stagnant sewage in front of his mother's apartment.
A city van inches through the gutted gravel parking lot
and the driver asks Elaine Norfleet whether she still has
power in the soon-to-be-condemned apartment.

"Yeah," she says, "we still have power."

And then she goes back to the matter at hand - how
to pay the funeral home the $701 and change she still
owes. Talk is cheap, but burying a 13-year-old boy isn't.

– *March 19, 2000*

A Third World Man
Dies in a First World Town

❄

The machine is a Brower Packer bobbin stacker, and it shut down for 18 hours last weekend after they pulled him out from under it, eyes wide open, barely breathing, already cold.

It was Saturday evening before his older brother got Cone Mills Corporation's permission to climb the stairs in the old White Oak denim plant and see where it happened. By that time, the machine was up and running again, and there was a woman doing Mahamadou Na-allah's job.

It's not a difficult job, but it's critical. On the stacker sits a bin that gradually fills with empty bobbins the doffers remove from the yarn-spinning machines. If the bobbins aren't returned quickly enough to resupply the spinning machines, that can slow down production.

Which is where the operator comes in – throwing the switch on the hydraulic lift. It tips the bin full of bobbins into a hopper that feeds them through a conveyor system, to be neatly stacked and returned to the machines that spin 24 hours a day, except maintenance every other Sunday.

As for Mahamadou Na-allah, 33, who died last weekend after apparently getting caught under the bobbin stacker, Cone Mills didn't give much detail. And maybe that's understandable.

He started as a temp last spring. He was from Africa – nobody at the mill could say which country – and he didn't speak much English. Neither did some of his co-workers on the "D" shift. When the police answered the 911 call, a technician recalled, they needed a translator for the Hispanic workers.

And that's the way it is in the neighborhood on an eastern tip of Greensboro, where Na-allah shared an apartment with three other men from his native Niger. In the parking lot, a neighbor takes a quick inventory, pointing door to door: African. African. Spanish. Spanish. Indian. African.

On the Cone Mills ID badge Na-allah's brother retrieved along with the keys to his Toyota, the face in the photo looks familiar. But I doubt we crossed paths.

He worked 7 p.m. to 7 a.m., and on days off, usually wound up going in for the overtime. In two years in the U.S., he'd never gone to the movies or to a club. He cooked his meals at home, packed his dinner for work, bought his clothes second-hand at a thrift store.

Why should I spend money on clothes? he once asked his older, taller, more sophisticated brother, Salifou, who had gotten after him about it. I don't have anybody to visit here. I don't have a girlfriend.

He sent money home to his wife and three children in Niamey, the capital of his native country in the southern Sahara. And that was his life – work, rest, phone home to Niger every few days, work some more.

Until last Friday, when the police came knocking on Salifou's door, saying there was an accident and Mahamadou "didn't make it." Nobody saw it happen, the managers said, and the medical examiner has yet to give a cause of death. The OSHA investigator signed off on the machine that same day, and the work goes on. For now. But climb the worn wooden stairs to the spinning room, and there's an atmosphere of weariness, of futility about the 97-year-old plant. It's the sign outside the employees' gate that lists "Hours Worked Without a Disabling Accident." It's the 1,000 or so parking spaces they don't need anymore, since the jobs went south, or east.

It's the people with seniority hanging on at Cone's last Greensboro plant, and its last unionized plant, because the money's still decent. But they're face to face with the writing on the wall – working alongside immigrants from the very Third World countries where the jobs inevitably end up. Newcomers like Na-allah – late arrivals to the table just as the meal is ending.

Last week, Cone sold its headquarters building. And just so you realize it's not only Cone: Across town, Guilford Mills had announced that it would close its original plant and move another 400 jobs to Mexico. The reason, it went without saying, was Asian competition and dirt-cheap labor, and the news came from Chuck Hayes himself – the former CEO always known for his bravado and salty language. Somebody said he had tears in his eyes.

But as for Mahamadou Na-allah, he's buried an ocean away from his wife and children, in a Muslim cemetery that's hard to find unless you know it's there. According to Islamic practice, the funeral was before the second sundown, last Sunday.

Of course by that time, the Brower Packer bobbin stacker had been up and running for a shift or two, and someone else was doing his job.

– August 6, 2000

Heavy Lifting: The Death of a City Day Worker

❄

He died in the line of work last week, and when his fellow city employees crowded into St. James Baptist Church for his funeral, they came straight from the job without time to change out of their uniforms.

No dress blues, no white gloves, but the gray work clothes and orange T-shirts of the Greensboro solid waste worker – 146 men and one woman who pick up the trash, leaves, brush, old sofas, washing machines, and whatever else we put at the curb.

Stephen Antwoine Allen, crushed after falling off a garbage truck that was backing up a street at 7:40 last Monday morning, 30 minutes into its route, was working an entry-level job the city can't keep filled, even in a tight job market.

It's the job of the pick-up man riding the back of a rear loader, and for nine hours at a stretch, jumping down to heft broken furniture, tree limbs, cans of yard waste – anything up to 50 pounds, the brochure says. Then again, who reads the brochure?

"It's a hard job and a stressful job, and you've got to be in shape," said Tim Gant, 34, a heavy equipment operator. "Cold weather and rain is the worst. No, take that back. Being out in the heat is the worst."

Steve Allen, 25, reminded Gant of himself when he first came to work for the city – a likable young man trying to get a foot in the door, adjusting to the sudden prospect of being a father. Allen, a temporary solid waste employee since the summer, has a child on the way, and was working on his GED.

"He was trying to get it together, and I think he did get it together," said his father, Louis Allen, who said his son had often skipped from job to job.

"I told him if he would just hang in there a little bit this time, he would get hired permanently. And he was showing up. He was there every day. That counted for something."

Until Allen could qualify for a commercial driver's license, a requirement for a permanent job with solid waste, he worked there as a temp through Ready Staffing. The agency, a short walk from the Patton Street garage where the city trucks leave at dawn every weekday morning, is paid $8.39 per hour for each worker it sends the city.

How much of that $8.39 goes to employees like Allen seems to be a mystery to managers both in solid waste and purchasing. Both departments said they've never asked that question – and a Ready Staffing supervisor wouldn't tell me.

But it's no mystery to Allen's co-workers.

"Temps get about $5 to $5.25. They need eight or nine hours to get $40 a day," said bulk trash driver Keven McNairy. "That's before taxes."

It's the legacy of years of prosperity: Fewer people line up to do the tough, physical jobs, and there's higher turnover for those who do. Try riding the back of a manual trash truck for nine or 10 hours, anyone will tell you, and it's OK for the first week.

"The second week, you're going to be sore," said Jeryl Covington, director of Environmental Services, "and the third week, you might be thinking of getting another job."

The other side of the coin is that the volume is higher – people throwing away mattresses, TVs, dishwashers, buying new ones. With this kind of equation, where do workers like Steve Allen fit in?

"A little kid came up to me the other and said, 'Hey garbage man!'" said Charles Williams, 33, who worked on a rear packer and is training for an automated truck. "And I thought, well that's OK. Then when I got home, my little girl called me that, too."

Nobody sees the other things they do – using their radios to call in car wrecks and break-ins, or sensing when something's not right on their route – for instance, an old man abruptly stops putting his barrels out.

Things get taken for granted until they're gone. But the man on the back of the truck isn't taken for granted – at least not by his co-workers, who come to the funeral straight from the job, without time to get changed.

– November 4, 2001

Tempus Fugit:
The Old Grandfather Clock

❄

The grandfather clock James Adkins built keeps perfect time, on one condition.

It's nothing you can see from the outside – not the polished oak cabinet, not the rotational face that goes from a picture of a deer standing in a forest over to a sailing ship at the full moon. No, the secret is inside where the weight is – chimes, gears, delicate cogs that run their precise course if you adhere to one simple rule. That is, you leave the clock where it stands and never try to move it.

And the thing is, James Adkins, 89, has never been tempted to move it. He built this house on the gravel road back in 1938 for $500 – the poured concrete porch, the labor, everything. He's never been to the beach, unless you count Okinawa. Never drove a car that wasn't a Plymouth – unless it was a Dodge. Never voted any way but Democratic – except for a county commissioner one time.

And all these years as the clock ticked away in the stillness of his parlor on Craddock Road, he's never wanted any woman but Martha. He met her at a country dance up the road when they were teenagers, and 70 years ago last week, they ran off to Danville and got married.

Seventy years, and Martha remembers their first fight, which unfolds not long after the ceremony in Danville. She's neatly made their bed when he carelessly tosses his hat on top. She picks it up and throws it on the floor. He stomps on it.

So after an icy breakfast, Martha's mother has to know: It's none of my business, but what in the world is wrong with you and James? To which Martha replies, He's just got no sense.

It's one of those petty arguments that seem to happen in winter, especially with the 16 inches of snow they had that winter. And of course, they apologize.

But it makes you wonder. What's the glue that keeps a marriage in one generation going, solid as the old wooden chest at the foot of James and Martha's bed, while marriages in the next generation split apart so quickly?

They never had a honeymoon, so the only wedding picture James and Martha own is two cameos that a portrait studio put together for them in a frame.

On the other hand, they've got a shoe box full of fragmented snapshots that come later in the family tree. There are '60s prom pictures snipped down the middle to edit out the estranged parties. There are '80s school pictures of the granddaughter who came to live with James and Martha after her parents divorced. And for her part, the granddaughter is now divorced twice herself, and raising a son she had by a third man.

And there again, how do you measure generations against each other, like columns in a ledger, deciding which one is "the greatest," as James and Martha's generation has been called, and which the "slackers?"

In Martha's way of thinking, you can't compare them.

They're both standing in different places, with their own sets of hardships.

For instance, James worked 45 years at the same furniture plant, turning down every promotion, but always making it home in time for dinner, which Martha had on the table by 5:30 sharp.

In the meantime, their son is a boiler room supervisor who works at all hours, carrying a walkie-talkie when he's at work, and wearing a pager when he's not. And then there's the granddaughter they raised, a single mother now raising a son of her own, working third shift on weekends to save on child care during the week.

This year, she scraped together a down payment on a double-wide. Seeing as she now had a permanent place, James gave her the "grandmother" clock he'd made for her in his workshop.

It's smaller than his, with a cherry wood cabinet and a face engraved with the Latin phrase "Tempus fugit." Time flies.

But just like the grandfather clock that ticks along in the stillness of James and Martha Adkins' parlor, it measures neither years nor generations. All it counts is a single moment in a stationary place.

— December 31, 2000

PART 5

The Eve of St. Agnes, the Shortest Day of the Year

A World of Pain:
The Ballad of "Johnny Blaze"
❄

Cop reporters call these stories "briefs" because, I suppose, there's not much to say.

At 1:30 a.m. the Saturday before Thanksgiving, a man walks out of Spoony's Bar on South Aycock and gets shot five times after an altercation. There's a parking lot full of witnesses, but they are reluctant to cooperate. Et cetera, et cetera, you can hear yourself say. End of story, right?

Well, not for Johnny Junior Ellerbee – a.k.a. "Johnny Blaze" – the 22-year-old street dealer who finds himself lying on the pavement with five large-caliber holes in him. Two in the arm, one in the chest, one in the back as he tries to run.

They take him to Moses Cone, stitch him up, give him who knows how many pints of blood. But that last bullet, in the spine, turns out to be the problem. Nobody says so when he wakes up the next morning, not directly, but Johnny can connect the dots.

How many steps does he have on his front porch? one of the doctors asks. Wheelchair ramps, somebody suggests. Finally, he hears that word. Paraplegic.

Him, Johnny, on the street since he turned 16, quit high school, and struck out on his own, living in motels, or at women's apartments, or in jail from time to time – drug charges, weapons charges, and that first-degree murder case they dropped for the time being, for lack of evidence.

And wouldn't you know, the same Greensboro detective gets his case. He comes up to his hospital room to get a statement, and it ticks Johnny off: *I'm gonna work on this case just as hard as I did trying to put you away the first time.*

Johnny just sits there. What else can he do? They've got him propped up in a wheelchair, big plastic breastplate strapped on him, and every day a friendly, soft-voiced therapist comes in to lift his numb legs, an exercise he's had to do since his "accident," as she calls it.

He's paralyzed from the waist down, but his legs are still muscular. And with his hair in cornrows, you can still glimpse the gangster pose he might have struck when he worked the corner at 1500 McConnell Road, near the infamous Lincoln Grove neighborhood.

Not that selling crack is all he's ever done for a living. He used to raise pit bulls for profit – loyal, affectionate dogs unless you show them otherwise – and he could make $1,500 on a litter.

But raising dogs means vet bills and dog food, and only so much demand. So with a 4-year-old daughter for Johnny to support, selling crack is a more dependable job. Though it does have its stress and its occupational hazards. There's no failure in the crack business. Just prison or death.

So Johnny lives by the rules of the trade. Don't sell drugs where you lay your head. Limit how many people know the spot where you stand. Most important, never go unarmed – which is what this incident before Thanksgiving was about.

See, Johnny's .45 had been stolen, and he'd broken the jaw of the man who stole it. Which brings us to that night at Spoony's – a sports bar Johnny didn't normally frequent – when the two men meet again.

It's a small world, and a small town, which lends itself to certain – well, ironies. Just ask Detective R.E. Edwards. In 1997, he charges Johnny with first-degree murder in a robbery gone awry. Then, the Monday before Thanksgiving, he's assigned to find out who shot Johnny.

He calls me back on his day off, while he's watching his family trim the tree. Sure, he agrees, it's a strange turn when one of your usual suspects is now a victim. But there's no poetic justice. Just the faces of the young black men, a whole sea of them, the detective has watched go to the grave or to prison.

Sometimes he wishes he had a snapshot of every one. Lying in some parking lot in a pool of blood. Or caged up in the penitentiary for 21 hours a day. Or wearing a colostomy bag, because a gunshot tore through the organ that used to handle that.

He'd show the snapshots to the first-timers, the wannabes, and ask them: Is this what you want to be? Or how about this?

Johnny, however, knows better. Nobody leaves the street life until they have to. And when a young thug of 14 or 15 gets a gun in his hands and the "rah-rah" in him, you can't tell him anything.

And now, at the age of 22, Johnny Junior Ellerbee, a.k.a. "Johnny Blaze," is neither in prison nor in the grave.

He's somewhere in between, back where he started. Lying in a room at the same hospital where he was born, waiting to go home with his mother.

– December 3, 2000

Homicide Shift:
Quitting the Last Cold Case

❄

When you leave the department after enough years, enough homicides and headlines, you don't leave without your badge. They mount it on a plaque that you can take home and hang in the den. For a dollar, you even get to keep your gun.

So when Detective Dave Spagnola walked out of the Greensboro Police Department on New Year's Eve, the day of his retirement, and looked back at the drab '70s outline of City Hall – a new building when he came on as a rookie – it wasn't like the movies. No violins played in the background, no well-rehearsed voiceover ran through his head, explaining what this moment meant.

It was just the close of business, the end of a very long shift and a parade of faces, gradually fading. A few were culprits, like Horace Beech, the crazed-looking drifter convicted of killing those old women. Most belonged to victims. Serine Whittle, a big story at the time. Sadie Farmer. Ed LeBrun. And all those drug murders, open and shut, whether or not they had enough to go to trial.

Even Dung Duc Vo, the Vietnamese jeweler killed in his shop on Spring Garden, is due to be avenged one of these days, whenever they get around to serving the warrants Spagnola filed in the 1991 robbery.

No, the ghosts that haunt a person aren't the ones that have been put to rest. So the ink is dry for Spagnola, the book is closed. That is, unless he happens to drive by the North Church mini-market that used to be the Circle K. Especially on a winter's day.

❄ ❄ ❄

Something always lingers in the air at a crime scene, and it stays there, frozen, until whoever is in charge takes down the yellow tape and lets it go, returning to business as usual – in this case, a convenience store.

First is the smell of burnt coffee. Beneath that, of course, is the smell of dried blood, a lot of it behind the counter where clerk Eugene Pierce has fallen dead, shot in the eye, once again in the skull, still clutching the dollar bill the killer had handed him.

But there's something else lingering over the scene, a sixth-sense feeling, a jolt of fear and pain, a shudder of desolation.

It might be the impact on the murder victim, a 19-year-old A&T student filling in for a friend, ringing up a candy bar one minute, dying on the floor the next.

It might be the fact that someone who is cold and soulless enough to do such a thing has just been through here, breathing this air.

Whatever it is, it makes the hair stand up on the back of Detective Dave Spagnola's neck. This is one of his first homicides. And looking back on it, Dec. 9, 1989, is a perfect day for a murder.

There is snow on the ground, and the roads are slick. Things are slow. Nobody is likely to get in the way of a holdup – least of all, the old lady with the walking cane who lives in the apartment building across the street.

She's standing at the counter waiting to pay for her Pepsi and cigarettes and sees the whole thing happen before she gets shot in the neck, falls and plays dead. Even after she recovers, she will be too afraid even to look at a photo lineup of possible suspects. Her doctors rule out hypnosis.

Outside, there are footprints in the snow. Hundreds of them. Like the rest of the evidence in this case, they lead everywhere and nowhere.

The police search the rooftops and storm drains in case the killer threw away the gun. Then again, why would he? There is no surveillance camera, so they go through the cash-register tape, running down every customer who has been in, every bag of M&Ms sold, every can of Vienna sausages.

The $5,000 reward Circle K puts up keeps the case alive, at least in the back pages, but the tips don't pan out. Not the Post-It note somebody drops on Spagnola's desk, saying he ought to take a look at a Pizza Hut robbery in Hickory because it involved a .32. Not a schoolgirl's third-hand report that someone saw two men going into the Circle K that day and remarked that "they have guns."

So it's stone-cold, a whodunnit, maybe the worst kind for a detective: Some blameless person shows up for work to do a job and gets murdered by a stranger.

The stranger has done this before, judging from the way he tries to eliminate the witnesses. He gets away with it. He'll do it again.

❄ ❄ ❄

Last night's lecture to his teenage daughter was the automatic teller card. Every month, Spagnola warns her, there are two or three cases of a woman being abducted and forced to withdraw money using a card. So she should hide it in the car somewhere, he says, and not keep it in her purse.

Sunday afternoons, he usually winds up checking on her at the little eatery where she works behind the counter. He doesn't like the layout, to be honest. There's no escape route from where she stands. He gets her to move a freezer case.

It's a handicap, knowing the things he knows. But once it's in there – the final look on a murder victim's face, the smell of bone dust in the autopsy room – you can't extract it like a sore tooth.

He's sitting in a Tate Street coffee shop the week

before his retirement, going over the Eugene Pierce file. He's barely aware of his own gaze, following a customer who looks like a college professor. The customer hands the cashier a dollar bill, takes his change and leaves. Spagnola goes back to his file.

It isn't like the movies, or "C.S.I.," where forensic science catches the bad guy in 60 minutes, minus commercials. It's an imperfect world, random, unfair.

He wonders about Eugene Pierce, a student from New Jersey whose parents sent him to college in Greensboro, where he would be safe. Had he seen the short, dark barrel of the gun? Did he think about grabbing it?

Spagnola flips past the photo of the Circle K in the snow, hopelessly ringed by hundreds of sets of footprints. One of them belongs to the killer, but the closest Spagnola ever gets is a feeling that makes the hair bristle on the back of his neck as they put up the yellow tape.

Now, the time has come to let it go, to get back to business as usual. Before long, his daughter will be leaving for college. But not UNCG. They've got the perfect program for her, but it's too close to home.

– January 4, 2004

The Question Was: Who Shot Mouse?

❄

The final note in Autopsy Number B99-0572 is what they call the "summary and interpretation." It's the part that explains how the man on the table in the yellow paper hospital gown got here.

Gustav Sidney Brown, it begins, was a 23-year-old black male ...

A microscopic exam reveals no pathological abnormalities, the doctor writes. This was a well-nourished, well-developed young man who had all his teeth, no prostate problems or gallstones, no traces of cocaine, alcohol or heroin in his blood.

Duly noted on the diagram is an abdominal tattoo that says "All Eyez On Me," the name of a Tupac Shakur CD. And like the rapper, killed in a drive-by shooting in Las Vegas, there's not much doubt about what killed Gus Brown.

The cause of death in this case, the medical examiner concludes, is a gunshot wound in the head.

❄ ❄ ❄

It was clear as day. It was, in fact, daylight on Reid Street, one of the usual-suspect back streets off East Lee that looks much the way it did on March 26, 1999, except for some vinyl siding that has spruced up the dingy frame houses, covering the bullet holes.

Everybody saw it happen, or nearly saw it, even Gus' brother William. A green car slowed to the curb. The driver said something through the open window, then pow-pow-pow-pow-pow and sped off.

By the time Gus' mother drove from her home a mile away, the paramedics were cutting away his clothes.

The evidence people were careful to write it all down on the inventory, along with the $10 bill that slipped out of his hand as he fell: Perry Ellis boots, Tommy Hilfiger jeans, orange Adidas hooded sweat shirt, Clench 701 ball cap.

Finally, there was the expensive yellow and black leather Avirex racing jacket – the one that would figure into the case – lying there cut in two.

So maybe it was a mother's instincts, about to be rendered useless, that made Annetta Dilworth do what she did next.

She stooped and started gathering up her son's clothes, picking up after him one last time. The police officers shouted to her. This is evidence! She let it drop back to the pavement.

> *"You're nobody/ 'Til somebody kills you."*
> - The Notorious B.I.G.

The preacher at the funeral wondered out loud about the mystery of why these things happen. Then he gave an answer the mourners had heard before, at how many funerals for young black men, brothers, cousins, playmates they'd known since kindergarten? Young black men, 15 percent of Greensboro's population, and 65 percent of the homicide victims in a typical year.

"Maybe if this gets one young brother's attention," the

preacher said in his strong, practiced cadence, "it will serve a purpose."

Annetta Dilworth didn't hear him. She didn't hear much that day. With her gaze fixed on Gus in the open casket and the suit she bought him to be buried in, her mind was blank one instant, flooded the next. Everything was disconnected and out of sequence, like a deck of cards fluttering in the air.

She saw Gus as a little kid – they called him "Mouse" because he was small. Smart but always in trouble at school. She saw him the day he got out of prison, trying to work a regular job, frustrated when he got fired, telling her, I tried it your way, now I'll do it my way.

There was the handmade card he sent her from prison on Father's Day, the sentiment catching her by surprise ("Because you've been a mother and a father to me," he wrote.) The unexplained trips to New York and Florida. And that voice talking to him on the phone, as she listened on an extension:

Man, I can set you up.

Nothing connected until they were leaving Bethel A.M.E. Church, and the pall bearers she'd asked to carry her son's casket had been replaced. The new ones had been handpicked by a Southside drug dealer. He stood back from everyone else, unapproachable, in charge. She didn't know the face but never forgot that voice:

Man, I can set you up.

Afterward, when everyone gathered at the family's home, the dealer gave mourners rides in a rented limo, champagne, anything they wanted. Like it was a party. Like it was the prom. Young women posed for pictures, hands on hips, right out of Bonnie and Clyde, or some gangsta rap video.

Annetta was beside herself, but her surviving son, William, pleaded with her in the kitchen in a way that made her listen. *Don't say anything. Please.*

Everything was beyond her control that day, except for one thing. That was when Gus' young son Hakeem, just 6, stood beside the casket and touched his father's face. It was cold. Hakeem took off his tie and laid it on his father's coat.

A swoon cut through the room, broke the spell of the gangsta fantasy, and somebody said to Annetta, Go get him. Take Hakeem away from there.

It was the one thing she had control of that day. She stood her ground. Leave him be, she thought. Let them see what they've done.

❄ ❄ ❄

"If people understood me, I wouldn't be here now."
- Gus Brown, age 11, to a school psychologist

A smiling, outgoing, attractive youngster," the psychologist wrote of the 9-year-old sent by his mother to Chapel Hill for testing. Attentive, eager, an "exceptionally good" vocabulary.

Then what was the problem for Gus Brown?

Surely the answer would be here, in this thick stack of papers in storage at the Guilford County Schools, between the pages stamped "CONFIDENTIAL" and "FOR PROFESSIONAL USE ONLY," the CAT, Wechsler Intelligence Scale, Bender-Gestalt Test, Children's Manifest Anxiety Scale.

But it's one contradiction after another. He tests a year above his grade level in most areas but misbehaves in class.

His kindergarten teacher calls him a "happy, active child." By third grade, his teacher warns that he "does not always apply himself." In middle school, he gets an "E" in science and a "D" in social studies. By seventh grade, a science teacher says he has the intelligence to perform at a high level, but his attitude and conduct are "poor."

By that year, seventh grade, he has switched schools 10 times, his mother is married twice and divorced twice, and is herself going to nursing school at night and working during the day. The school system passes him along, but for a summer school session or two, where it's noted "Gus participated in all class activities."

By the time Gus turns 14, Annetta enrolls him in ninth grade at Smith High School, where he makes straight "F's." After he's caught joy riding in a stolen car, it's one last try at state training school. This backfires: While he's there, he meets a girl from Greensboro and gets her pregnant.

His next stop is prison, for violating his probation. Gus is a man now, on his own.

At the County Farm, at age 18, he talks to older cellmates about how to set up a drug house, find someone to verify your employment, sign a lease.

But it's just a jailhouse fantasy. True, the money is good – even better than the welding apprenticeship his mother tried to get him into – but the thing is that you work 24 hours a day. Nobody lets you sleep, he tells his mother, and they're always smoking and drinking.

One night, he's been to the dealer's condo off Bridford Parkway – classy on the outside but squalid inside, unbelievable, wall-to-wall people.

That does it. Two more weeks, he vows, enough time

to get some cash for Hakeem and the baby brother about to be born, and Gus is going to walk away from this whole thing.

❄ ❄ ❄

It's a new set of faces these days on Reid Street, but the story hasn't changed.

On a warm afternoon, a glowering, shirtless young man sits on the porch at 816 Reid, every few minutes trotting to the curb to lean in a car window.

Across the narrow street, an elderly man sits watching a grandchild play in his front yard. A drunk lurches around the corner at Bragg Street, toward Douglas Park, and a young man in a suit walks along Reid Street carrying a Bible.

"Are you ready to meet Jesus?" he asks.

This is where Gus Brown was shot after walking to his red Nissan 300ZX parked at the curb in front of 816 Reid St. – 5:39 p.m. March 26, 1999. By 8 p.m., he's declared dead, and now it's a homicide with one essential question: Who?

Inside the house that night, it's as if no one lives there – just a bedroom set, and a red light in one room. Two days before the murder, police had chased a suspected crack buyer into 816 Reid, and described what they found.

It was a typical drug house – little vials of crack, crack pipes, a police scanner radio, about $900 in cash stashed in videotape covers, nothing bigger than a $20 bill, but most of it in fives and ones. And finally, guns – Glocks, Rugers, a Smith & Wesson revolver. The police take it all.

The day of the murder, there are plenty of witnesses

who see the car speed away but nobody much interested in talking to the police. One exception is the lady across the street – she wasn't home at the time but has plenty to say.

Gus was a nice boy, she tells the officers. He always treated her with respect and made people move their cars when they were blocking her driveway. She hadn't seen this particular incident brewing, but she'd seen a lot on Reid Street.

"It makes me sick," she tells police. "Nobody can be so stupid that they don't know what's happening on Reid Street."

The why of it was the harder question for Detective Dave Spagnola, because everybody more or less knew who shot Gus Brown.

They dropped the charges against an Eastside drug dealer after a key witness developed amnesia. Or decided there was no future in telling the truth.

As for the motive – you could take your pick. One was a turf war between Southside crack dealers and an east side operation shot up days earlier.

Another story centered on the leather jacket Gus wore the day he died – in this version, he loaned it to a friend while they washed cars. Had the shooter mistaken Gus for the man who borrowed the coat?

It depends on whom you believe, if anyone. When the cops arrived at the shooting, everybody ran out the back door except one woman. She went out to hold Gus' head – and get the $700 in his pocket, one witness would tell police.

But the bigger question – the "Why" with a capital "W" – why a nice boy with brains and a good mother was hanging out on Reid Street in the first place, striking the pose, wearing the clothes – that's the part the detective doesn't understand.

Car doors locked, he rolls by the scene of the crime on Reid Street – busier at night than in the daytime – then turns toward MLK, every mile reminding him of one homicide or another, a less-than-scenic tour.

He thinks about this documentary he surfed past the other night on Discovery, where a herd of young male elephants gets cut off from the adult males, through some disaster or man-made calamity.

Left to their own devices, they run amok, destroying property, fighting each other, nobody with the strength and love to rein them in. Nobody knows how, now that a generation of adult males is gone.

But getting back to Gus Brown. What was the question?

※ ※ ※

All she knows is, she's starting all over again at age 48 – Pull-Ups and soy milk for her youngest grandson – he's allergic to milk – and grandparent-teacher conferences for Hakeem, now 9 and not having it easy at school.

After work at the home health aide company she started from scratch while her children were growing up, Annetta Dilworth waits for Hakeem's school bus at the after-school program.

It's the same play school where she used to drop off Gus and William back when she was in nursing school, and it all feels familiar to her. She asks Hakeem how his day was, trying not to be too easy with him, not to be too hard, then sees him off again for the afternoon.

He walks away, lugging his book bag, and she

motions him back with a silent reproach.

"It was nice to meet you," he says, shaking a visitor's hand.

Meanwhile, inside the darkened 2-year-olds' class, Gus III is napping, and dreaming dreams that nobody knows. He's one more boy without a father, and only the medical examiner to explain why.

"Gustav Sidney Brown was a 23-year-old black male who received multiple gunshot wounds."

— November 18, 2001

Class of '75: The Christmas Night That Time Forgot

❄

They were having another high school reunion this weekend – the big 30th for Grimsley's class of '75 – with cocktails on the roof of the Kress Building, dinner at the Empire Room, jazz on the lawn of a vineyard.

They'd no doubt bemoan the few gray hairs starting to appear, maybe trade tales of moving their oldest into the freshman dorm. But unlike past reunions, this time they didn't show the video of classmates who have died. It always put a damper on the party, seeing those faces again. Too much blast from the past. Especially one face that never changed from high school. It brought back memories of the first reunion they had – the Royal Villa Hotel, Christmas night, 1976. It was the last time any of them saw Joanne Bomar alive.

❄ ❄ ❄

They took Jody Boum's old green Chevy Nova. On the radio, "Blinded by the Light" was playing about every five minutes – an infectious song, even if you weren't sure what it meant. Who cared? It was winter break, they were going to a party for Grimsley seniors and graduates at the Royal Villa, and when Jody picked her up at the house off Hobbs Road, Joanne wore the boots she'd gotten for Christmas that morning.

The girls had stayed friends after Grimsley – Jody going to Lees-McRae, Joanne to UNCG. At 19, Joanne was shy and feminine in a sweet, funny way. For instance, when they stopped to eat – Joanne loved cheeseburgers so much that she would order herself two, then order two drinks, hoping the cashier would think the food wasn't all for Joanne.

The party that night was one of those loud, crowded affairs in the huge ballroom of the old Royal Villa off Randleman Road, and the guests kept ducking into upstairs hotel rooms they'd rented. Jody and Joanne went separate ways when they arrived, planning to meet later and go back to Jody's for the night.

But when it was time to go, Joanne was nowhere to be found. By 4 a.m., her mother called the Royal Villa, and later called the police. At about the same time, a blood-soaked car someone tried to push into the Dan River was found near the state line, and police outside Danville picked up a teenage boy walking naked on the 17-degree night, claiming to be Moses. His name was Dan Tidmore Brown.

❄ ❄ ❄

Prosecutors don't keep files this old, so when the Parole Commission notified Guilford County District Attorney Stuart Albright in June that a convicted murderer was about to be released, Albright went to the basement of the courthouse to look at the dusty clerk's files from 1976.

It was supposed to be a cursory task for the D.A.: Before he made the obligatory trip to the basement, he noted that by 2005 standards, a person convicted of second-degree

murder and given a "life" sentence would scarcely expect to
serve 28 years.

But when Albright opened the thick, dog-eared file on
the case and came to the autopsy report on Joanne Bomar,
he slowed down and read every word. Then he did an
about-face.

"She was brutally beaten to death, burned and possi-
bly raped," Albright later wrote to the parole analyst.
"Specifically, Mr. Brown struck her in the head with a tire
iron time after time after time. ..."

The June 15 letter went on, in words that don't get
much more graphic – words like "oozing" and "gaping" and
"pulp." But the Parole Commission, whose executive director declined to comment on the case, released Brown on
June 22, one week after Albright faxed the letter.

By law, the commission can only confirm that Brown,
who was 18 when he was arrested and is now 46, will
live somewhere in Guilford County. Brown didn't return
phone messages left at his family's home, so a 1994
prison interview provides the most recent comments he
made to the newspaper:

"I'm not that person anymore," said Brown, who con-
fessed to killing Bomar, a friend of his older sister, after
offering her a ride home to Hamilton Lakes from the
Royal Villa. Brown claimed he had experienced a "psy-
chotic episode" after taking a large dose of PCP, an animal tranquilizer that causes hallucinations.

Bomar's parents and brother, anguished at the way
she died, long since moved to South Carolina and, year
after year, would make the trip to Raleigh each time
Brown was up for a parole hearing.

Finally this spring, Bomar's mother, now a widow and
herself in frail health, was advised by a retiring parole

commissioner not to make the trip. After 28 years, the mother said she was told, Brown's parole was inevitable.

"I feel like I'm reliving the whole thing," Trudy Bomar said in a phone interview after the district attorney's office recently sent her a copy of the old file, containing gruesome details of the crime that never emerged when Brown pleaded guilty.

"Time goes on, but it doesn't 'heal all wounds,' " the mother said. "Time doesn't heal anything."

❋ ❋ ❋

Years turned into decades, maybe the same way they do in a prison cell. But out here, they crept up on the Class of '75 – first the 10th reunion, when people still tried to impress each other and look successful, then the 20th, when they at least wanted to look thin. By the 30th, it doesn't matter anymore. You are who you are. And all of us here knew you when.

Jody Boum finished college, moved away, went to work, got married and had a daughter. But all this time, she never really stopped thinking about Joanne. You see, she went to the courthouse back then, at age 18, and read that thick file, thinking somehow that she could have prevented this if she'd left the party with Joanne.

These days, she'll be watching Montel or Oprah, a story about crime victims, and that triggers it. Or if she has the radio on and hears "Blinded by the Light," although she doesn't hear that song much anymore.

One time, back in the '90s, at a catering event, Jody looked across a banquet hall and there was this girl who was the image of Joanne – her eyes, her hair, the shape of her face. Unable to take her eyes off the girl, Jody finally walked over.

Do you have a sister? Jody asked, remembering that Joanne was adopted, wondering if it could be. But it couldn't be. The last time she saw Joanne was 1976. Everyone had changed since then, gone on living – the Bomar family, Jody, the Class of '75. Even the killer, Dan Brown, was middle-aged by now.

Time only stood still for Joanne. It has since Christmas night 1976.

– August 7, 2005

Boy Meets Girl, Man Loses Woman

※

The other day he plays his first round of golf in 14 months – everybody says it will do him good, he says he needs to hit something – and out on the green it sinks in.

For the first time in 14 months, he's not needed. There's nothing more he can do for her now.

Steve Foskett, 40, has the raw, out-of-sync look of a man whose wife has just died, and died at 34. Brilliant, love of his life, high soprano at church.

One minute she's acing her pre-med exams and doing her hospital training hours at Moses Cone, the next minute she's collapsing right there on the hospital floor in something called a "grand mal" seizure, which is just as bad as it sounds.

They go back and forth on the diagnosis, but the bottom line is a grade-four brain tumor, which is practically inoperable and growing fast. Doctors never say never, but Steve knows in his gut there isn't much time.

Now, there are any number of ways that any number of men would assess this particular situation. One would be to walk away. Or run, Steve knows. Head straight for the beach at Key West.

But first you have to know Steve. He's from Michigan, he's a lawyer, not exactly a Hallmark kind of guy.

In the 10 years they've been married, and the five they dated before that, he's maybe bought her two or three pieces of jewelry on Valentine's Day. Not that Kim wore jewelry much. Just kept it in a special place in her jewelry box.

They met at Chapel Hill, him in law school, her in business, which she turned out to dislike. At a softball game one day, he throws his arm out and this tall, pretty girl comes over and starts rubbing his arm. Hmm. I could marry this girl, he thinks, and eventually he does.

And that's the way it is for Steve. He's lucky. He gets a law practice going in Greensboro, no trouble paying his bills, and cruises along with not many bumps in the road.

Sure, his dad died back in the '70s, but it was a heart attack and then he was gone. Otherwise, Steve's lived a boy's life – he keeps up with his cases, goes to play golf, she does her thing, they meet at home.

That is, until the day after the seizure, when the doctor comes in with the test results. Steve takes off his glasses and buries his face in his hands. Thinking, wasn't it just about five minutes ago that he was still in high school?

Then an amazing thing happens, the first of many. There's a hand on his shoulder – Kim's – and she's smiling at him. It's all right, she says, don't worry about it. How does a man walk away from that?

And for the next 14 months, there's not a tear, not a complaint from her, as bad as things get. What the drugs don't take away, the biopsy and last-ditch surgery do. Piece by piece, she loses Chapel Hill, then pre-med. Then loses her speech, her ability to use the bathroom or get dressed. By the last week, she can't swallow anymore, then on Wednesday at 3 a.m., she stops breathing.

Between Faith Wesleyan Church and Kim's Weaver's Guild, people were always there to help. Which amazed Steve, the way people came out of the woodwork.

But a lot of it fell to him, and there was another source of amazement. He discovered that this was better than sitting on the beach at Key West – just being here with this woman, watching Jay Leno, sleeping in the same bed, or eating breakfast.

Now, the morning after the first full day that Kim is gone, Steve wakes up on the futon in the living room, because he can't sleep in the bedroom.

His thoughts bounce around the room. He realizes everything in this place is hers, except for his two guitars, and the one of two cats that turned out to like Steve.

He remembers how she made him paint these walls three times before he got the right shade of blue. He's thinking about dropping the divorce part of his law practice. Tired of listening to people argue about who gets which TV.

Then he gets dressed and goes to play his first round of golf in 14 months. And he loses badly, and he doesn't care.

– February 15, 1998

Miss Eva's Cure:
Vinegar, Honey, Price is Right

❄

S o there she is in her early 40s, that first year after Junior got killed, and it actually crosses her mind while she's driving on the interstate.

Holly Knight doesn't have a soul – mother dead, father long dead, no brothers or sisters, and now her husband killed in an accident at his job site.

Anyway, the car is getting up to 80, right along those concrete barriers, and she catches herself thinking. All it would take is one jerk of the wheel, and you wouldn't have to do this anymore.

Missing him this way, first thing in the morning, last thing at night, everything in between. That landlady pestering her at all hours. And Holly dragging herself to work third shift at the same hospital where they took Junior.

When the doctors came out the day he died, Junior's best friend sat there and cried out loud. He didn't even cover his face.

So the next thing Holly knows, she's sitting at a rest area near Statesville with the engine still running, her heart pounding, shaking all over at what she almost did before something stopped her.

No, several things stopped her from jerking the wheel. She realized she might take another driver with her. Or wind up paralyzed, like the patients in the neurological ward. And finally, she remembered Miss Eva's hair appointment at Mother and Daughter Salon. Holly had promised to drive her.

And so she pulled herself together, got back on the interstate, and never said a word about it when she got to her mother-in-law's house and drove her to the beauty parlor.

Now, Miss Eva, Holly's mother-in-law, is a whole different story. And not one you'd necessarily read in the paper. Or include in one of those oral history collections, like the one at the Greensboro Public Library, the one where they now need "ordinary" people.

Because in all her 92 years, Eva Moore hasn't done a single thing that you could call extraordinary. She grew up on a farm near Big Creek, raised five sons on her own, buried two husbands, survived two wrecks and gall bladder surgery, worked at Blue Bell sewing back pockets on men's overalls, and at Bates Nitewear sewing piping on collars.

And when she wasn't at the factory, she was priming tobacco, always with a baby at her feet, hers or somebody else's. Get to the end of the tobacco row, move the baby over, start on the next row.

She was one of 12 children and stepchildren, but she's the only one still alive. It's hard to keep track of what happened to every one of them, although losing her son Junior isn't anything she'll soon forget.

You see, it's one thing when the old ones die. But your own child. And so quickly – a dump truck backed over him at the construction site, and he lived long enough for his wife, Holly, to get to the hospital.

The two women hardly knew each other until that

day. Until Holly just couldn't go back to their trailer, except to feed the dogs. She couldn't go back that day, or the next, or the next.

And so she stayed with her mother-in-law, a 90-year-old woman with a crooked back and a sore shoulder, who swears by one remedy for any ailment: Two tablespoons of honey mixed with a tablespoon of White House apple cider vinegar.

Holly would work until 7 a.m., and by the time she'd get home, Eva would be having her coffee in her nightgown, reading Ann Landers, the horoscopes and the obituaries. On her old TV with the rabbit ears, they'd watch "The Price Is Right" and Eva always guessed the answers. They'd watch "Judge Judy" and "Judge Jerry," Eva always siding with the man getting sued, no matter what.

I guess you could say they grew on each other. Every Saturday, Holly would drive her to Madison to get her hair done and shop at Dollar General, Eva's favorite store. Every Sunday, Eva would cook – biscuits, steak and gravy, pound cake – and always make too much.

And when you can't quite decide what the moral of the story is, there's only one way to find out. You stick with it, and that's what Holly did. This past Friday, she turned 46, and got a card from Eva, probably from the Dollar General.

"To my daughter-in-law," it began, and Holly skipped past the printed sentiment to the bottom. In Eva's spidery, scratchy hand, she'd written: "I love you, love you, love you, love you, LOVE you."

And signed it, "Your mother-in-law."

– October 1, 2000

Sister Gabriel
and the Perpetual Adoration

❄

The rule is that the chapel never be left empty. Someone must be present every minute – at the height of the workday, or in the dead of night, when the only sounds are the swish of the furnace and the chime that marks the hours.

And like the old, ornate silver setting that holds the Eucharist in the chapel at Maryfield, the nuns who started this place came from across the Atlantic. As their thanks to U.S. troops in World War II, they wanted to serve the poor and the sick and were offered the Penny Mansion, a big stone house that had been deserted and last used as a High Point nightclub.

So the group of young Irish nuns cleaned up the beer bottles, the red tablecloths splattered with candle wax and, 60 years ago, took a leap of faith. With no money in the bank, no backing, they opened a nursing home.

Hard to imagine against the backdrop that is Maryfield today – an army of bulldozers carving out a sprawling, well-heeled retirement community complete with a beauty salon, heated pool and clubhouses that serve salmon for lunch. Once, this was the fledgling mission of a small group of nuns including Sister Gabriel Ahern, a County Cork native who died last month at age 86.

In those days, they lived on the grounds in a small

house that had once been a stable. Sister Gabriel slept in an attic, cold in winter, hot and close in summer, and her job was to feed everyone.

Feed them she did – at the original, 22-bed home and through two subsequent expansions that turned the place into a large, modern nursing home. Regardless, she was the first one up in the morning, turning on the warmers and the big gas range, and the last one to bed, after taking a staff member with her down to the basement to check the boilers every night, never going alone.

She scrubbed the pots and pans, mopped the floors, put up the stock and cooked from scratch – no cans, no processed food, no cookbook. They picked strawberries  in summer and snapped green beans on the porch. And for any resident who didn't like what was on the menu?

"She would send a big pot of hot oatmeal down the hall in the morning – she called it 'porridge,'" recalled Hazel Greene, a nursing assistant here since 1972, "and a big pot of soup every night. It was whatever they wanted. And it was wonderful."

In 1964, cook Billy Hairston was only 14 when he came to work for Sister Gabriel, a sturdy, strong-willed nun who did not believe in short cuts.

"God will know in the end," she would warn in her lilting brogue, as she taught Hairston the old-school way of doing things – Christmas puddings that took days to ferment, twice-baked potatoes that never came out of the freezer.

There was rarely a weekend off, and what was left over in the kitchen, she would load into the car and deliver to needy families, always taking a helper, never going alone.

But as the years passed, even Sister Gabriel slowed down, became forgetful and finally went to live in the nursing home herself. For as long as she could, she would try to help. Sometimes she would sit with another old Irish nun who came to Maryfield to retire, Sister Kathleen Clarke, if only to hold her hand.

Early on a Sunday morning, she asked for a cup of tea, said she was "ready" and died. The next day, Sister Kathleen, 85, died, too, and after the bishop said a funeral Mass in the chapel, they were buried in two plots behind the old stone mansion, where the mission started out 60 years ago.

It was as if Sister Gabriel waited for someone to come with her. She never went anywhere alone.

— December 31, 2006

PART 6

Christmas Morning

The Lasting Gift of Puppy Love

❄

He was not the smartest dog in the world.

Nor was he the dumbest.

That distinction would always belong to the first beagle my parents adopted, a dog who successfully defended his title long after he'd gone to that great rabbit chase in the sky.

And when I saw a film clip of the president the other day with his new dog, I suddenly understood one of the great mysteries of my childhood.

Whatever had possessed a strong-minded woman like my mom, who had begun every day of her life since I'd known her with just one vow – "I will never get another beagle" – to inexplicably cave in without even a whimper? And most bewildering of all, for it to be nobody's idea but her own?

This week's clip of the leader of the free world, obliviously cradling his new friend, explained it all. He had succumbed to the most powerful temptation on earth – more irresistible than wealth, fame, romance, even the elixir of power itself.

As with the president, my mom fell prey near Christmas. She was shopping at the mall when she let my younger brother, a preschooler at the time, tug her by the skirt into the pet shop.

While my brother was looking at iguanas and parrots, mom caught the puppy out of the corner of her eye, or maybe he caught her. Either way, what ensued was your classic beagle moment. The kind that takes years to undo.

There he was by himself in a cage with just a plastic water dish for a toy. Mom drew closer, already in a beagle trance, and he sat up straight. He had silky, oversized brown ears, white chest and muzzle, and a wet black nose.

He seemed about to let out a small woof, but this he suppressed. The brown eyes – glistening, soulful and profoundly melancholy – said everything he needed to say.

In a nutshell, they said that a couple of weeks from now, children all over New York would descend sleepy-eyed to their living rooms and behold what was under the tree. Children just like her son. But of course, the beagle recognized, her son no doubt already had a dog. And so the puppy would just have to spend Christmas in an unlit pet shop at a cold and deserted mall, with nothing to play with but his empty water dish.

And looking back on it, that was the last smart thing Grover ever did.

For the moment, Mom managed to collect my little brother and get out of the pet shop, but already it was too late. When my dad got home she told him about the poor little puppy at the store. He looked at her as if she were out of her mind.

Which of course, she was. Or perhaps oblivious is the word – oblivious to everything she knew that bringing home a beagle meant. Our previous beagle, dearly departed Clay, was a slave to his hound instincts. When he caught the scent of a rabbit, for instance, Clay would follow the trail for days until he was exhausted and near blind. He'd seek out cow pastures, rolling and reveling in the pungent manure, then come home badly needing to be bathed.

By Mom, of course.

So my dad shrugged in resignation and the next day met my mother at the pet shop to see the puppy. When Mom saw the sign on the cage, she looked stricken: "It says he's 'SOLD'" she read in disbelief, but before she could confess her secret relief, Dad had more news.

"That's right," he said. "He's sold. Sold to YOU."

Now, living in a more rational age these 25 years later, everybody knows the perils of puppy love, especially at Christmas. We've been educated about it, like trick-or-treating or undercooked poultry.

Pet adoption specialists such as Randy Barrow, who runs an Oak Ridge farm for greyhounds retired from the races, carefully screens would-be greyhound owners before any hound leaves the farm. It's a long-term commitment, he explains, not something based on a moment's infatuation. And this, of course, coming from a man who takes in 50 greyhounds at a time.

My mom, on the other hand, is cured. The only beagle in her house is an inch-high ceramic one that's been dropped and glued back together a couple of times. And whenever anybody reminisces about what a lovable dog poor Grover turned out to be – however stubborn, inept and useless in other respects – Mom has the last word.

"I will never get another beagle," she says. "And this time, I mean it."

– December 12, 1997

For the Kid Who Doesn't Want Anything

❄

This is just her third Christmas, but one look at Suzzy's list for Santa and I can only conclude that, despite my best efforts, she's not watching enough TV.

These are her dream gifts, in order:

1) "A green whistle."

2) "A ride on a big green bus."

3) "My toy pumpkin full of candy from Halloween."

Now, other than the candy, which is bad for her teeth (and which I finished off more than a month ago), it's not an unreasonable list. She might even get two bus rides. The trouble is, her grandmothers are asking for gift ideas.

"Oh, she'll like anything," my husband tells them. "But nothing that talks and nothing 'interactive.'"

Nothing annoying, is what he means. Like the musical choo-choo train one of us bought my sister's son 20 years ago. It played little plastic discs, and each piercing tune ended with a long, shrill steam whistle. That is, until the discs mysteriously fell down the heat vent and melted. And before we could buy replacements, the train itself got crushed by an automatic garage door, a freak accident witnessed only by my sister.

But 20 years later, walk the aisles of any big toy store and you realize that the musical choo-choo was just the beginning.

Once you eliminate the talking toys, the interactive toys and the purely annoying toys, all that's left is the Pokemon version of "Sorry!" and a 500-piece jigsaw puzzle of Leonardo DiCaprio standing on the bow of the Titanic. Which, on second thought, are both annoying.

But the fundamental problem isn't that a lot of toys on the market grate on adults' nerves. The fundamental problem is, they're no fun.

Take Talking Tonkas, a new twist on the sturdy dump trucks and bulldozers. Touch any moving part on Chuck the Firetruck, for instance, his sound chip plays a message. But how many times can you hear, "My ladder's ready for action!" or "Water on! Glug-glug!" before you get bored? Or accidentally leave Chuck in the path of the automatic garage door?

More passive still is the electronic Tender Sounds 'n Motion Nursery. It's a deluxe set of baby doll equipment including a monitor that makes the cradle rock when the baby's sound chip emits a cry. It's the ultimate toy – it plays all by itself.

Even the participatory board games don't show much flair. With notable exceptions such as "Whac-a-Mole" – the object is to hit a plastic mole on the head and set off the arcade lights – most are cheesy merchandising spin-offs.

There's the junior version of "Who Wants to Be a Millionaire?" The trivia game quizzes players on sports, science, music, movies and (surprise) TV. (Sample question: "Who is the host of TV's No. 1 smash hit game show?")

Likewise, there's a "Survivor" game "based on TV's hottest real-life adventure show." There's an "Anastasia" game, spun off the story of the Russian imperial princess as told to Disney. There's even an "NSYNC Backstage Pass Game." To win, you elbow your way through the crowd, get past the security guard and meet the four-inch cardboard cut-outs of Justin, JC, Lance, Joey and Chris IN PERSON!

Not that some toys don't appeal to the imagination, but you have to wonder how they would look sitting under the tree. For instance the "Official Police" play set (comes with riot gear and handcuffs), the anatomically accurate "Human Torso" for ages 8 and up (bonus instructional CD included) and the "Synthetic Frog Dissection Kit" ("Looks and feels real!")

And if it's true that children learn through play, there are entire lines of toys to prepare them for lives of conspicuous consumption. We're not talking about pedal cars anymore, but $500 battery-powered Peg-Perego cars and Harley-Davidsons.

Nor do you have to settle for a simple tool box and workbench – you can get the complete Home Depot line of power tools and accessories for the future do-it-yourself homeowner.

Meanwhile, pint-sized homemakers are no longer limited to the Easy Bake Oven. Now, there's a whole miniature kitchen: refrigerator, dinette, coffee maker and Farberware pots and pans. Not to mention a choice of three upright vacuum cleaners – Little Tikes, Hoover WindTunnel or a Dirt Devil that "really picks up."

Hmmm. It really picks up. And when you stop and think about it, an actual working vacuum cleaner could enhance Suzzy's small motor skills and grasp of cause and effect, even while appealing to her need for imaginative play.

Now, if they could just come out with a good steam iron in her size.

– December 8, 2000

Uh-oh, It Snowed

❄

Just me and you/ Doodle-y, doodle-y doo.
- from "Jay Jay the Jet Plane"

There are only three words in the language that can motivate a man to shovel an ice-encrusted driveway down to bare cement, before he's even had his morning coffee:

SCHOOLS ARE CLOSED!

Hearing that Hindenburg-scale news flash the other day, my husband sprang into action before dawn, determined to be the first one out of the house.

He'd slept in his long johns the night before and left his galoshes by the bedside with the pants sticking out of them, firefighter-style.

Ever since the last snow day that he spent home alone with two children under the age of 6, he'd been drilling relentlessly for this moment. Each night, he hefted 10-pound containers of Quick-Melt like bar-bells, meticulously sharpened the blade of his ergonomic snow shovel and practiced, while blindfolded, squirting de-icer into the locks on his car doors.

And now, as the closings at the bottom of the TV screen began to show how dire an emergency this really was – threatening to shut down everything from the ABC stores to the South Lizard Lick Clip 'N Curl – all his training would be put to the test.

"Out of my way, woman!" he shouted as he raced past me to the door, snatching an ice scraper out of my hand. "I've got to get to work! They're going to be swamped!"

Now, this last statement was pure speculation, seeing as he works in sales – and not sales of generators, snow plows or Christian Brothers brandy. But as I watched him frantically chip away at the frozen hulk of a mini-van, something told me this was an act of survival.

What told me was a voice, and not a little voice. It was the voice of Mickey, age 4, barreling down the halls of our split-level house with all the projection of a young Marlon Brando as Stanley Kowalski.

"Mom-AAAAAAAAY!" he boomed from the top floor. "Suzzy's squishing me against the ceiling."

From the background came peals of laughter from Suzzy, 5, lacking his projection, but still outweighing him.

"I am not," she said, and just then her laughter changed to howls of pain. "Ow, ow, OWWWW! He just hit me behind the glasses."

Now, I'm no fountain of wisdom, but I know not to get in the middle of an internecine squabble, particularly at 6:30 in the morning. With their nutritious breakfast of Cap'n Crunch with Crunchberries kicking in, what they needed was a distraction.

"Hey!" I said, "Want to play with your new toys?" To which they answered in unison, "What new toys?"

Actually, I had been hiding these toys since Christmas, waiting for a rainy day, or at least, a day that I didn't plan to be home.

Out came the Rock Star Karaoke with the Britney Spears cassette. The battery-operated Hot Wheels track that flings the cars through a figure-8 with life-like

NASCAR sound effects. And the Barbie of Swan Lake Unicorn & Carriage, which doesn't make any sounds, but is just really annoying.

Not that the snowy outdoors couldn't be hours of fun. Or at least minutes, as it had on Sunday – Mickey demolishing each attempt at a snowman, Suzzy bundled so tightly she couldn't get up from making a snow angel, and finally just lay there whimpering. All this flashed before me as my husband headed out the door, saying the most unrealistic thing anyone ever says: "Maybe you can just work at home today."

But moments later he was back, mission aborted. He stooped painfully at the waist, using his ergonomic snow shovel as a cane and muttering, "Ergonomic my @#%$."

When I got home from work that night, I followed a trail of damp mittens and snow pants upstairs. He was sitting by himself, wearing Prince Daniel of Swan Lake's plastic Tudor crown, and staring, trance-like, at an episode of "Jay Jay the Jet Plane."

"Jay Jay and Big Jake have just learned a lesson in honesty," he said catatonically, not even looking up.

"Great," I answered. "And were you able to get some work done?"

– January 28, 2004

Airport Layover:
The Face You'd Know Anywhere

❄

A ll I had was her airline arrival time, and when I got to the crowded terminal an hour late, I had a problem.

I didn't know what Beth looked like anymore. I hadn't seen her in 20 years, and the only picture I have is from junior high, way before she left New York for Denver.

But that's still the face I see when we call each other every couple of years, and that's the face I pictured as I read the e-mail last week. Pressed for time. Will explain later. Have a three-hour layover in Charlotte. Could you drive over?

And that's the face I find myself searching for in the milling crowds on the concourse. The problem is, I'm looking for my 15-year-old friend from junior high, but Beth and I are over 40 now. What are the odds we'll find each other?

Now, I don't know if you've been to the Charlotte airport lately on a weekday morning looking for a face in the crowd you may or may not recognize, and who may or may not recognize you, but it's a lot like your first day at junior high.

If, say, you missed the bus, lost your class schedule and locker combination, went to the wrong building, didn't know a soul. Pressing against a tide of strangers who all seem to know where they're going, you strain to

hear garbled announcements from the main office ...
Paging U.S. Airways passenger Bess Castlebaum. Please
pick up the nearest red courtesy phone for a message.
"It's BETH KOPPELKAM," I tell the operator. "Can
you try again?"

I hurry from coffee shop to cocktail lounge, looking for
a lone woman traveler with long hair – no way she'd cut it
– and I gamble on the smoking section. I spot a 40ish
woman who could be the face 20 years later, but she's
drinking iced tea. Not likely. She smiles warmly. No chance.

I bypass the newsstand racks of glamour mags and
romance novels. She didn't go in for cheap sentiment,
and in all the years I knew her, I never saw her cry. Not
over some guy. Not in the vice-principal's office. Not
even the time we cracked up her dad's Pontiac, and she
had to work at Burger King to pay it off.

Which, in hindsight, made it noteworthy that she
scraped up the money to visit after I moved to North
Carolina in 10th grade. I didn't know a soul in the whole
state, let alone my high school, and I must confess. That
face was a sight for sore eyes.

But we hadn't kept up. We didn't send Christmas letters like the one Beth got from a mutual friend ("It was
FIVE PAGES LONG") and reading my byline on the
Internet wasn't her idea of a thrill. ("Like I've got nothing better to do.")

Of course. What was I thinking? People move on. You
can't go home again. And just when this airport rendezvous
seemed not just unlikely to happen, but like tampering with
destiny if it did, I heard the garbled announcement over the
P.A. system again. Only it was reversed now.

Will the person who paged Beth Canofspam please
pick up the nearest red courtesy phone ...

I walked about a mile before I found a phone, and somebody was using it. Lo and behold, it was the face, plus 20 years.

"Is this the nearest red courtesy phone?" she said glibly, then steered me to the bar where she had a tab going. She'd spent the first half hour looking for me, and the second half hour looking for people I might mistake for her.

So what brought her back east? The high school reunion a couple of weeks ago? "Are you KIDDING?" Beth said. "I don't think I'm on their mailing list."

Once, she and some friends wrote a pact on a matchbook to meet at a Long Island park in 2000, which was a long way off. By the time 2000 came, they forgot all about it.

No, she was visiting her dad. It turned out her mom had died in May at 70 – one day fine, next day a heart attack.

"You think you have all this time," Beth started to say, and I thought she was going to cry but she didn't. "It's like I said when I gave the eulogy. My mom was always 39, so when people ask me how old I am, I say, 'My mom's 39. YOU do the math.' "

We talked about life's mysteries – men, baldness, body piercing, '70s bands that are back on tour. Then it was time for her flight, and we had to rush to the gate.

She showed her boarding pass, started down the walkway, then turned: "I love you," she said, and then the face was gone.

So as I pull out of the parking deck, a group of girls walks toward me four across, obliviously blocking the road. In my head I hear this wisecracking voice I've heard since I don't know when, since I found my first friend at junior high: Take your time, I've got nothing better to do.

Did the voice belong to me or to the face? After all these years, it's hard to say.

– August 27, 2000

Cut the Chain:
The Girl Who Handled Snakes

❄

The last time I saw Myra Anne, she was in the rutted stretch of middle age. A course of inevitable sameness that less surprising people resign themselves to, on the numbers alone.

After all, she was living in the same state where she was born 55 years ago; same city, 34 years; same house on Chestnut Street, 27; same job, 17.

Work dried up, and she was doing temp jobs, getting headaches, downsizing to an apartment, shuttling on weekends to Hilton Head, where her mother was dying a lingering death.

Then one strangely balmy afternoon in late 2005 she called on me, but not with news I was expecting.

"I'm joining the Peace Corps," she said as we stood under the bare oaks at UNCG. "I don't know where I'll be assigned, but I leave next spring."

The next time I saw her was last week at Starbucks on Battleground, home for daughter Lara's wedding. She was tan. She'd gotten younger.

"You know how I got these muscles?" she said, rolling up a sleeve over a bicep. "Laundry. I do my wash in a bucket. I ride my bicycle two miles a day past a fishing community. I eat brown rice and buy vegetables from people who grew them."

Her assignment took her to a place I had to look up. Suriname is a small country above Brazil where they speak Dutch, and mix cultures from Javanese to Creole to Maroon. She does blood pressure screenings, and helped convert a deserted hospital wing for labor and delivery.

It's a total culture clash. In the coastal capital, they drive on the left. But where she spent 15 months in the interior rain forest – a four-hour ride in flat, narrow boats – there are no roads at all.

The heat makes August in Greensboro feel mild. Sweat runs in your eyes, and it's so humid that a pair of shoes not worn for a day sprouts mold.

Myra Anne slowed down. She breathed in the air and saw things. Scarlet Rode ibis and leatherback turtles. Women in the village pounding out a bread called "kasava," wearing costumes for the national emancipation day called "Keti Koti" – translated as, "cut the chain."

And I guess I've heard these before-and-after stories of midlife reinvention before. A fellow reporter quit the paper to join a mission in Haiti. A Habitat friend taught English in Mongolia, and now Africa. Even the doctor who delivered my two children into the world – and me to the path of minivan-driving dependability – turned 50 and chucked it all to practice in Cuernavaca, Mexico.

But the thing about Myra Anne is that she's always been one to tell the middle part of the story. It's the part where one decides to cut the chain.

The departure point was a Miami hotel, her Peace Corps staging area. A friend dropped off Myra Anne, and three pieces of luggage.

"If I call your cell," Myra Anne told the friend, "you have to promise to come back and get me, no matter

how close you are to North Carolina."
She never made the call. And last week, she had
already left again when I realized I needed a photo. So
her daughter, Lara, who looks like a 28-year-old version
of Myra Anne, brought me two: One from the wedding
party, but the other, her favorite.
It's from around 1970 outside the dorm at UNCG.
Myra Anne, like every biology major, had to pose with a
boa constrictor. And there was a time when I wouldn't
have recognized the girl in the picture.
Now, I realize I've met her. Just last week at
Starbucks.

— September 2, 2007

A Cowboy Dream, from
a Cradle Endlessly Rocking

❄

Why my mom hangs onto that old crib was always a mystery. Until now.

It's been wedged up there in pieces under the rafters, in a remote corner of the attic, taking up space for the longest time. It's not even the kind of crib people use anymore, not like the gleaming white crib given to us second-hand for young Suzzy the spring before last, a crib that looks like something out of a storybook.

No, the crib in the attic is light-brown rock maple, circa 1948. It used to have a blue and white decal of a cowboy losing his hat on a bucking bronco, but that rubbed off years ago. The side panel doesn't slide up and down anymore, and the rails have deep white gashes left by five teething babies, and eight or nine grandbabies.

Even the bars look too far apart, enough for a baby's head to get stuck in. A Consumer Product Safety Commission recall just waiting to happen.

But I have to admit, puffing my way up the attic stairs last weekend, it's a good thing my mom held onto the old crib.

Ahead of me, my brother teeters along the beams between billows of pink insulation, past rows of Samsonite suitcases we've lost the keys to, boxes of faded prom pictures, an unused wooden wine rack somebody made in shop class.

I stand marooned on a sheet of plywood while mom waits at the foot of the stairs.

"If you lose your balance, you'll come right through that ceiling," she warns me, palms outstretched, as if ready to catch my nine-months-pregnant frame if I fall.

"Here it is," my brother shouts, holding up a section of the disassembled crib, a side panel with swirly bars that look like posts from a merry-go-round.

As we lug the pieces downstairs, Brian pauses over one with a metal rod and a rigid, inch-long spring on it.

"Remember this?" he asks, eyebrows arched, and with a flick of his wrist sets the old spring spinning along the length of the metal rod.

Of course, I remember. In fact, I can't remember anything before it – a nameless, endless, mindless game that pre-dated checkers, marbles, blocks, even walking. The crib is our own random cultural artifact, flotsam from the usual make-do American voyage – upstairs, downstairs, across the hall and back – that has no end.

First it's upstairs – a flat on 77th Street in Brooklyn's Bensonhurst. Actually, not an apartment as such, just the upstairs of my grandparents' house, converted for my newlywed parents.

And my grandparents' house is in reality a "semi-detached" – in the other half lives an uncle who followed them from Italy. As for the nursery where the crib first lands, with my brother in it, it's a hallway outside my parents' room, with a Venetian blind to keep out the light. Cozy, my mom calls it.

Hardly a year goes by and another baby in a second crib is lined up in the hallway. They move downstairs when the third baby comes – smack in the middle of a

June heat wave – and the kids sleep in the old dining room, the parents on a Castro Convertible sofa.

My turn in the old cowboy crib comes when we move to the roomier Long Island suburbs, where I'm born on Thanksgiving night. I graduate to a twin bed and a remodeled room, but the crib isn't retired just yet.

A fifth and final baby comes at 5 a.m. on New Year's Day, 1965, while the doctor and nurses grouse about the hour, and even my now-seasoned dad questions whether it's really – really – time to go to the hospital.

So here we are again in January 2000, expectantly dusting off the old crib, and it's like rubbing the genie's bottle. Out come the labor stories, same as the babies – one after another, with no rhyme or reason to their unexpected twists and turns.

Like the time, my mom claims, that lime-green hospital Jell-O sped up her delivery. Or when somebody forgot to put gas in my brother-in-law's car and they got stuck on the way to the emergency room. Or the night my sister demanded not only anesthesia, but a blindfold.

They're stories that are short on clinical details but long on close calls, dumb luck and the utter mystery that runs through every family saga you ever hear.

Like the mystery of who, precisely, forgot to put gas in the car. Or how you fit three babies in the hallway of a quarter of a house on 77th Street. Or how Mom knew that after 52 years, she ought to hang onto a rock maple crib with two generations worth of teeth marks for a while longer, just in case one last cowboy comes along.

Now if I can only find a blue and white decal of a rodeo rider on a bucking bronco.

– January 9, 2000

From Lowly Seed, Sturdy Vines and Sweet Fruit Grow

✳

Even if you don't believe in miracles, you have to believe in a 27-pound-12-ounce cantaloupe. There's not much choice.

Paul Lopp grew it right there in the courtyard at Abbotswood Retirement Community, where we were sitting around the other day waiting for the winner to be announced in the guess-the-weight of the cantaloupe contest.

It was parked on a platter for all to admire – big as a Thanksgiving turkey, enough melon ball potential to feed all 150 residents – and Lopp freely shared the secret to his success. Give it plenty of sunlight, water it every day, and resist the urge to pluck it off the vine too soon.

Where did he get the seed?

"Well, that's the funny part," said Lopp, 81. "They give us fruit to eat here – usually cantaloupe – and I found a seed on my plate. And I said, 'I'm not gonna throw this away, I'm gonna plant this seed.'"

He told me about the three children he put through Davidson College, about the job he once had selling Cadillacs and Packards until his doctor advised him to change careers, about the granddaughter who likes horses. Then he caught himself.

"I'm talking too much," he said. "But it's just so good

to have somebody to talk to again."

I thought back on a recent conversation I had with a Greensboro reader, Geraldine Whalen, who had been trying to get the community at large to visit people in nursing homes, maybe a rung or two up the care ladder from the more independent residents of Abbotswood. Whalen was having no luck, always getting the same basic response: "It's just so depressing."

Human nature, I guess, not to go opening doors without knowing what's behind them. In my case, they were the doors to a home for people with Alzheimer's, a place I drove past on a hundred Sundays without ever wondering who was inside.

Even after my Dad moved there this spring, my weekend visits were straight to his room, with no more than a few quick hellos to the staff and his neighbors. But that changed in the last two weeks of his life. Short visits turned to long vigils, and I began to see the place in a different light – in the quiet routines of weekday mornings, early twilight and the wee hours.

One night in the corridor outside Dad's room, I heard a young nurse's aide softly singing – "You are my sunshine, my only sunshine" – and one by one, voices of residents along the hall joined in.

Another day, I saw an old woman sitting on the floor, chiming in a sing-song, little-girl voice, "Can I sit under the shade tree?" to a childhood playmate only she could see. And even in the sadness of this lonely disease, there was a hopefulness about this place you couldn't miss.

I don't mean hope of being cured. I mean hope that life still has meaning, and that human connection still has power – enough to take away the heaviness and dread I once felt walking through those front doors.

A case in point was the night my father died: The first person to console my Mom wouldn't be one of her kids, or the nurse, or the home's director, but a sweet, confused, old lady from Lewisville who had moved into the home the week before.

Now, I can't tell you on what level the lady comprehended what was happening, but she instinctively threw her arms around Mom to comfort her just the same.

The funny part, as the Cadillac salesman at Abbotswood might say, is that Dad wasn't gone more than a week before Mom was walking back through those doors as a volunteer at the place, listening to this person's worries, walking that person around the patio, feeding somebody else lunch.

Mom, a woman who devoted all her time to her family, now felt related to a family much bigger. And when someone new moves into Dad's old room the first of the month, I have no doubt Mom will visit that person, too.

So I don't know if that's what people mean when they talk about miracles, or if miracles come in different sizes, the way cantaloupes do.

But it does make me wonder. The same as that 27-pound-12-ounce melon and the man who grew it. A man who was a stranger to me five minutes before, inviting me to drop by any time, and telling me the secret to growing cantaloupes.

Not much to it, he said. Just plenty of water and light, and enough time to ripen on the vine. And the funny part is, any seed will do. Even the one on the plate right in front of you.

— September 13, 1998

Winter Solstice: Stirring Among the Bones

❄

This stage of a garden is called the "bones."

Which is not to say it's dead.

No, at Cove Creek Gardens, it's merely what remains after butterflies and blossoms are scattered, and the leafy excess of the equinox makes its garish, dramatic, over-the-top exit.

Now, everything is quiet. So quiet that a sparrow darting among the dry vines, ferreting out a brilliant red sparkleberry, makes a rustling that sounds like an animal many times its size. Above the smooth, far-off sound of traffic on Summit Avenue, five miles northeast of town, it's still enough to hear a woodpecker knock on a hollow tree. From the stalks of Chinese banana trees, the giant leaves hang in brown ruins, like sails of a tall ship that's been plundered and burned. By now, the lily pond has iced over a night or two. Somewhere in the depths, the goldfish are slowing down, ready to begin their long wait.

But this is no dainty Southern garden that closes for the winter. There's no sign asking visitors to excuse this season of repairs, no apologies for inconvenient frosts and rains that make TV announcers frown.

After all, we're in the high Piedmont, Zone 7, where the winter reaches down to 8 or 10 degrees on occasion, because it's supposed to. This is somewhere between the paralyzing deadfall of West Virginia, where garden founder Nancy Cavanaugh was born, and Cove Creek designer Julia Blizin's native St. Petersburg, where the tropical Florida jungle never sleeps. It just gets bigger.

Here in the middle, winter is the time for rethinking things, for poring over catalogues of possibilities, and taking up the mistakes that have been made in spring and summer – the reason for the heavy pruning that intern Michael Raburn performed on a cold Saturday morning in the high hedges of what designer Blizin calls one of the "rooms."

In fact, there are 13 rooms in the English-style cottage garden Blizin and Cavanaugh began 30 years ago – wisteria trained to the shape of tree trunks, native ferns, creeping raspberry, false indigo, mother-of-thyme.

The tiny seeds are harvested and collected in paper bags. The only way they can propagate is if they first dry out in a cool, dark place.

Meanwhile, the big hardwoods – the red oaks and Carolina hemlocks – use this barren period to put water back in the ground. Even the ice storms that in the past year or two felled the big hickories helped the garden, opening up places for new growth.

Everything here has a purpose, and the purpose is to perpetuate the cycle, to allow the garden to continue. But in winter, the garden rhythms go mostly unseen – except to Guenevere, a watchful tabby cat sitting perched beside a rain barrel. Nearby, a mysterious predator is about to devour its victim – a carnivorous "pitcher plant" has trapped a bug in the bottom of its spout.

As for human interest in nature, it might be called "deciduous" – it falls off in autumn and doesn't return until spring. Even then, we go from one climate-controlled bubble to the next, shunning anything other than room temperature, out of sync with the turning all around us.

For instance, the night earlier in December, when there was an unsteady feel in the air, Julia Blizin walked down to the field that leads to an unnamed branch of Buffalo Creek. In the moonlight, two weather fronts were moving toward each other, one warm, one cold, churning in a vast clockwise motion, a dance with the potential for vast conflict.

The next morning, Blizin walked among blossoms on the camellias – an odd, unseasonal sight. She stopped to study them a long moment, then made a note in the garden journal she keeps, rarely missing a day.

That's because even in the bitter chill, even on the shortest day of the year, there is something blooming, withering or stirring among these bones.

– *December 26, 2004*

About the Author

Lorraine Ahearn has worked for daily newspapers for 25 years as an investigative reporter and projects writer, first at the Annapolis Capital, and currently at the News & Record in Greensboro, N.C., where she was also metro columnist for 12 years. A native of Huntington, N.Y., she is a Phi Beta Kappa graduate of the University of North Carolina at Greensboro, where she holds degrees in English, French and Liberal Studies.
Visit her at lorraineahearn.com

About the Illustrator

John Hitchcock owns Parts Unknown, The Comic Book Store. In 2006, he was nominated for the prestigious Isner Award for "Dear John, The Alex Toth Doodle Book," an illustrated book of correspondence between Hitchcock and longtime friend Toth, the legendary artist and Hanna-Barbera animator. The book is considered to be the definitive book on Toth and his work. Hitchcock, an authority on the history of comic books, North Carolina Tar Heel basketball and professional wrestling, is a Greensboro native and graduate of Greensboro College, where he holds a BFA in painting.
Visit him at partsunknown.net

Acknowledgments

Thank you to the News & Record and John Robinson, Editor, for graciously allowing these stories to be reprinted, and to the editors who so patiently helped me develop my columns over the years: Betsi Robinson, Teresa Prout, Susan Ladd and Bill Hancock.

Thanks to my colleagues at the paper, past and present, for their creativity, know-how and good cheer, especially Elaine Shields, Jennifer Burton, Mike Kernels, Herb Everett, Lynn Hey, Nancy Sidelinger, Diane Lamb, Elma Sabo and Margaret Baxter.

Thanks to Alan Brilliant of Glenwood Community Book Shop for his knowledge, encouragement and support of Greensboro's writers and readers.

Thanks to the News & Record subscribers, who in one manner or another suggested many of these story ideas, and who with their generous feedback make writers better.

Praise to the only moral authority proven to teach children to survive deadlines intact. Thank you, Mom, for everything I have.

To Suzanne, Mickey and Kevin, you are my world!